CONFRONTING
YESHUA'S DIVINITY
AND MESSIAHSHIP

confronting issues series

CONFRONTING
YESHUA'S DIVINITY
AND
MESSIAHSHIP

J.K. McKee

TNN PRESS
www.tnnonline.net

CONFRONTING YESHUA'S DIVINITY AND MESSIAHSHIP

Cover photos: Istockphoto

Published by TNN Press, a division of Outreach Israel Ministries
P.O. Box 850845
Richardson, Texas 75085
(407) 933-2002

www.tnnonline.net/tnnpress

originally produced by TNN Press 2012 in Kissimmee, Florida

Unless otherwise noted, Scripture quotations are from the *New American Standard, Updated Edition* (NASU), © 1995, The Lockman Foundation.

Unless otherwise noted, quotations from the Apocrypha are from the *Revised Standard Version* (RSV), © 1952, Division of Education of the National Council of the Churches of Christ in the United States of America.

table of contents

WHAT DOES THE SHEMA REALLY MEAN?

ANSWERING THE "FREQUENTLY AVOIDED QUESTIONS" ABOUT THE MESSIAHSHIP OF YESHUA .. 89

abbreviation chart and special terms

The following is a chart of abbreviations for reference works and special terms that are used in publications by TNN Press. Please familiarize yourself with them as the text may reference a Bible version, i.e., RSV for the Revised Standard Version, or a source such as *TWOT* for the *Theological Wordbook of the Old Testament*, solely by its abbreviation. Detailed listings of these sources are provided in the Bibliography.

Special terms that may be used have been provided in this chart:

ABD: *Anchor Bible Dictionary*

AMG: *Complete Word Study Dictionary: Old Testament, New Testament*

ANE: Ancient Near East(ern)

Apostolic Scriptures/Writings: the New Testament

Ara: Aramaic

ATS: ArtScroll Tanach (1996)

b. Babylonian Talmud (*Talmud Bavli*)

B.C.E.: Before Common Era or B.C.

BDAG: *A Greek-English Lexicon of the New Testament and Other Early Christian Literature* (Bauer, Danker, Arndt, Gingrich)

BDB: *Brown-Driver-Briggs Hebrew and English Lexicon*

BECNT: *Baker Exegetical Commentary on the New Testament*

BKCNT: *Bible Knowledge Commentary: New Testament*

C.E.: Common Era or A.D.

CEV: Contemporary English Version (1995)

CGEDNT: *Concise Greek-English Dictionary of New Testament Words* (Barclay M. Newman)

CHALOT: *Concise Hebrew and Aramaic Lexicon of the Old Testament*

CJB: Complete Jewish Bible (1998)

DRA: Douay-Rheims American Edition

DSS: Dead Sea Scrolls

ECB: *Eerdmans Commentary on the Bible*

EDB: *Eerdmans Dictionary of the Bible*

eisegesis: "reading meaning into," or interjecting a preconceived or foreign meaning into a Biblical text

EJ: *Encylopaedia Judaica*

ESV: English Standard Version (2001)

exegesis: "drawing meaning out of," or the process of trying to understand what a Biblical text means on its own

EXP: *Expositor's Bible Commentary*

Ger: German

GNT: Greek New Testament

Grk: Greek

halachah: lit. "the way to walk," how the Torah is lived out in an individual's life or faith community

HALOT: *Hebrew & Aramaic Lexicon of the Old Testament* (Koehler and Baumgartner)

HCSB: Holman Christian Standard Bible (2004)

Heb: Hebrew

HNV: Hebrew Names Version of the World English Bible

ICC: *International Critical Commentary*

IDB: *Interpreter's Dictionary of the Bible*

IDBSup: *Interpreter's Dictionary of the Bible Supplement*

ISBE: *International Standard Bible Encyclopedia*

IVPBBC: *IVP Bible Background Commentary (Old & New Testament)*

Jastrow: *Dictionary of the Targumim, Talmud Bavli, Talmud Yerushalmi, and Midrashic Literature* (Marcus Jastrow)

JBK: New Jerusalem Bible-Koren (2000)

JETS: *Journal of the Evangelical Theological Society*

KJV: King James Version

Lattimore: The New Testament by Richmond Lattimore (1996)

LITV: *Literal Translation of the Holy Bible* by Jay P. Green (1986)

LS: *A Greek-English Lexicon* (Liddell & Scott)

LXE: *Septuagint with Apocrypha* by Sir L.C.L. Brenton (1851)

LXX: Septuagint

m. Mishnah

MT: Masoretic Text

NASB: New American Standard Bible (1977)

NASU: New American Standard Update (1995)

NBCR: *New Bible Commentary: Revised*

NEB: New English Bible (1970)

Nelson: *Nelson's Expository Dictionary of Old Testament Words*

NETS: New English Translation of the Septuagint (2007)

NIB: *New Interpreter's Bible*

NIGTC: *New International Greek Testament Commentary*

NICNT: *New International Commentary on the New Testament*

NIDB: *New International Dictionary of the Bible*

NIV: New International Version (1984)

NJB: New Jerusalem Bible-Catholic (1985)

NJPS: Tanakh, A New Translation of the Holy Scriptures (1999)

NKJV: New King James Version (1982)

NRSV: New Revised Standard Version (1989)

NLT: New Living Translation (1996)

NT: New Testament

orthopraxy: lit. "the right action," how the Bible or one's theology is lived out in the world

OT: Old Testament

PreachC: *The Preacher's Commentary*

REB: Revised English Bible (1989)

RSV: Revised Standard Version (1952)

t. Tosefta

Tanach (Tanakh): the Old Testament

Thayer: *Thayer's Greek-English Lexicon of the New Testament*

TDNT: *Theological Dictionary of the New Testament*

TEV: Today's English Version (1976)

TLV: Tree of Life Messianic Family Bible—New Covenant (2011)

TNIV: Today's New International Version (2005)

TNTC: *Tyndale New Testament Commentaries*

TWOT: *Theological Wordbook of the Old Testament*

UBSHNT: United Bible Societies' 1991 Hebrew New Testament revised edition

v(s). verse(s)

Vine: *Vine's Complete Expository Dictionary of Old and New Testament Words*

Vul: Latin Vulgate

WBC: *Word Biblical Commentary*

Yid: Yiddish

YLT: Young's Literal Translation (1862/1898)

Introduction

The *Confronting Issues* series by TNN Press began in 2007, as a selection of small stapled booklets, comprising a rather forthright article or two produced by Outreach Israel Ministries and TNN Online. Today in 2012, because of the significant wave of changes and transitions occurring within the broad Messianic community, the *Confronting Issues* series is being retooled a bit, into small books, addressing some of the major debates of the day. It would be our hope and prayer that these new releases are able to interject a well-needed perspective into the conversation regarding the different topics of importance, offering fair-minded and constructive solutions, which carefully address the Biblical text, and can sincerely help Jewish and non-Jewish Believers in their walk with Yeshua the Messiah.

There is no more pressing issue for Believers in Yeshua the Messiah (Jesus Christ), than understanding who their Lord actually is. There are many statements appearing in the Apostolic Scriptures or New Testament, which give witness to who He is. Yeshua is the Word made flesh (John 1:1, 14), He is the Lamb of God (John 1:29, 36), He is One who had the audacity to say "before Abraham was born, I am" (John 8:58), and He is One "existing in the form of God" (Philippians 2:6, ASV). Yeshua is the Savior of the world, whose sacrifice for human transgressions provides permanent atonement and forgiveness. Yeshua the Messiah of Israel is the One "of whom Moses in the Law and *also* the Prophets wrote" (John 1:45). Yeshua the Messiah is One who the Scriptures definitely regard as no ordinary man, as He performed miracles, had control over the weather, and who was recognized as unique by the forces of evil. He is "the first and the last, the beginning and the end" (Revelation 22:13).

While there is much about the nature of the Messiah that is difficult for mortals to fully comprehend, He is portrayed as the One in whom "all the fullness of Deity dwells in bodily form" (Colossians 2:8), and He is "our great God and Savior (Titus 2:13). He is the prophesied Messiah of Israel, and He is God made manifest in the flesh. Recognizing Yeshua as God, and as the prophesied Messiah from the Tanach or Old Testament, are two concepts that have been under continual attack by many outside *and* inside forces in today's broad Messianic movement — and the attacks continue to grow in intensity. There are people who have been caught easily unaware by poor arguments against Yeshua's Divinity and Messiahship. **There are answers to the claims against these foundational truths that are available for those who need an immediate shoring up of their faith.**

Confronting Yeshua's Divinity and Messiahship has compiled a number of key articles that I have written for the TNN Online website over the years, which are intended to directly combat errant ideas that circulate here and there within sectors of the Messianic community. Common claims that are issued against Yeshua being the Divine Savior, and Yeshua being the Messiah, are directly responded to with poignant observations and exegetical detail. If you have been in a situation where a rogue individual you have encountered makes a statement or two against who Yeshua is, as communicated to us in the Holy Scriptures, then this publication should serve as some useful ammunition against those claims. The most frequent statements that one will hear, which are made against Yeshua's Divinity and Messiahship, are directly confronted and responded to.

J.K. McKee, Editor
TNN Online

Answering the
"Frequently Avoided Questions"
About the Divinity
of Yeshua

answering the claims of the anti-Divinity Messianics

Anyone who has surveyed the Messianic movement—whether it be Messianic Judaism, the One Law/One Torah sub-movement, or Two-House sub-movement—knows that it is very broad and diverse. There is a broad array of theologies and opinions evident in the Messianic movement, just as in Christianity or Judaism. There are those who are theologically conservative, and those who are theologically liberal. There are those who believe that God has the ultimate control over their lives, and those who believe that they can determine their own destiny and dictate to God who He is, ignoring His direction. There are those who think deeply, and there are those who think simplistically. There are those who let themselves be tossed and swayed by religious politics, and there are those who do not allow entangling alliances to have an influence over them.

Since the 1990s and 2000s, it is not surprising that an age-old theological controversy, going back to the Second and Third Centuries C.E., has arisen in the broad Messianic movement: *Who is Yeshua the Messiah (Jesus Christ)?* **Is He God—or is He just a human man?**

This has now developed into a debate that is not so easily delineated along any kind of denominational, organizational, or ministry lines, *as it affects everybody*. While various Messianic associations and ministries have rightfully taken strong stands against those who would deride Yeshua the Messiah as being the Divine Savior—the fact is that individual people who may attend congregations which officially affirm Yeshua as God, may themselves only think of the Messiah as a good man who was connected to God in a special way, or some kind of exalted supernatural being, yet ultimately created. It is certainly true that there are many Christian people who attend church every week, being members of denominations which officially affirm the Divinity of Jesus, who themselves do not believe in it and only think that Jesus was a good teacher. So, individual people denying Yeshua's Divinity is not at all an isolated incident, nor is it uncommon to the world of Christian religion, at least.

What can make things in the Messianic movement much different, though, is our relatively small size, and the fact that many sub-groups and cliques are becoming more and more reliant on promoting themselves by various modern communication media. It is very easy for an outspoken individual in the assembly, who does not believe that Yeshua is Divine, to cause quite a stir. In the past, this would have only taken place by a person passing out questionable literature on the side, not too different from a dealer offering free samples of illegal drugs. What happens now is usually seeing various opinions expressed via a personal blog page or YouTube channel. All too often, individuals are caught broadsided when various arguments are made or encountered, not quite knowing what to do. Too many can be persuaded, even if just for a little while, into thinking that Yeshua the Messiah might not really be God.

Sadly, too many of today's Messianic congregational leaders do not know what to do about this. And, given the fact that apostasy is indeed prophesied to be a sign of the Last Days (2 Thessalonians 2:3), people denying major tenets of our Messianic faith is something that we are all going to have to deal with in increasing numbers as the Second Coming draws nearer. Pockets of individuals here and there denying Yeshua's Divinity is sure to be followed by much larger groups, and in time it will be found in some Messianic congregations' leadership and whole ministries. Those of us who are true to what the Scriptures tell us about Yeshua the Messiah, however, **can have confidence that He is indeed the LORD God, and He is indeed Divine!** There are fair-minded, Biblically-rooted answers for the questions and criticisms being made. *You do not have to be broadsided by some of the main, yet decidedly weak arguments, that are being bantered around.*

Approaching the Debate:
Why does the Messiah have to be Divine?

The question of whether or not Yeshua the Messiah is Divine, God in the flesh, has been a cause of considerable debate and dissention in various periods, since His ascension into Heaven. The Apostolic Scriptures record ancient hymns and creeds affirmed about Yeshua by the First Century Believers themselves (i.e., Philippians 2:6-11; Colossians 1:15-20; 1 Timothy 3:16), some of which may have been formulated to not only make key statements about who He is, but also subvert errant ideas that had circulated in various sectors of the *ekklēsia*.

In much of theological study since the First Century and ministry of the Apostles, we encounter the views of people who strongly believed that Yeshua (Jesus) must be God, and that any diversion of believing that He is not God must be viewed as theological heresy. There are also those who have strongly believed that Yeshua was only a human man, that He had some kind of special relationship with God and was quite possibly even the Messiah empowered by God, but was never God in the flesh.

Whether Yeshua the Messiah is Divine is an old debate, and while there are discussions about what this group of Christian leaders insisted, or what that sect did—**this is an issue that ultimately tries a reader's loyalty to the claims of the Biblical text.** How Medieval Roman Catholic leaders handled those who they considered to be "heretics," for example, *should not* be what guides our thoughts about this issue. What should guide our thoughts about this issue is understanding the wide-sweeping Biblical ramifications of: "these have been written so that you may believe that Yeshua is the Messiah, the Son of God; and that believing you may have life in His name" (John 20:31). What matters for our deliberations is whether or not the Divinity of Yeshua **is a clear teaching of Scripture,** that the Divinity of Yeshua is something reflected in the testimony of the Apostles, and how the Divinity of Yeshua is something which affects our salvation.

As I approach the issue of whether or not Yeshua is the Divine Savior, my reasons for believing in His Divinity are firmly based within the text of Scripture. From Scripture, we see stated in numerous places that only God can save human beings from their diverse trials, and allow His people to enter into His blessed purpose for them. The LORD God explicitly claims that He is the only Savior (derived from the Hebrew verb *yasha,* יָשַׁע)[1] of people:

> "For I am the LORD your God, the Holy One of Israel, your Savior; I have given Egypt as your ransom, Cush and Seba in your place" (Isaiah 43:3).

> "I, even I, am the LORD, and there is no savior besides Me" (Isaiah 43:11).

> "Declare and set forth *your case*; indeed, let them consult together. Who has announced this from of old? Who has long since declared it? Is it not I, the LORD? And there is no other God besides Me, a righteous God and a Savior; there is none except Me" (Isaiah 45:21).

> "I will feed your oppressors with their own flesh, and they will become drunk with their own blood as with sweet wine; and all flesh will know that I, the LORD, am your Savior and your Redeemer, the Mighty One of Jacob" (Isaiah 49:26).

> "You will also suck the milk of nations and suck the breast of kings; then you will know that I, the LORD, am your

---

[1] "be saved, be delivered (Niphal); save, deliver, give victory, help; be safe; take vengeance, preserve (Hiphil)" (John E. Hartley, "יָשַׁע," in R. Laird Harris, Gleason L. Archer, Jr., and Bruce K. Waltke, eds., *Theological Wordbook of the Old Testament,* 2 vols [Chicago: Moody Press, 1980], 1:414).

Savior and your Redeemer, the Mighty One of Jacob" (Isaiah 60:16).

"Yet I *have been* the LORD your God since the land of Egypt; and you were not to know any god except Me, for there is no savior besides Me" (Hosea 13:4).

These verses from the Tanach (Old Testament) attest to the fact that the LORD (YHWH) Himself is the only Savior and Redeemer, as demonstrated by great acts of deliverance and victory for His people. The claim of Isaiah 42:51, for example, is most exclusive: **"And there is no God apart from me, a righteous God and a Savior; there is none but me"** (NIV). The process of being saved from the eternal punishment to be meted upon sinners, directly involves actions performed by God Himself.

The key to properly dealing with whether or not Yeshua is Divine, is with how He could possibly offer any person eternal redemption as Savior, if He were only a human man.

The Apostolic Scriptures (New Testament) surely affirm that Yeshua the Messiah is the Savior (Grk. *sōtēr*, σωτήρ). The angels proclaimed at Yeshua's birth, "for today in the city of David there has been born for you a Savior, who is Messiah the Lord" (Luke 2:11). The Apostle Paul wrote, "For our citizenship is in heaven, from which also we eagerly wait for a Savior, the Lord Yeshua the Messiah" (Philippians 3:20), and he spoke about "the redemption which is in Messiah Yeshua" (Romans 3:24). He further says, "In Him we have redemption through His blood, the forgiveness of our trespasses, according to the riches of His grace" (Ephesians 1:7; cf. Colossians 1:14), which is undeniably the activity of salvation. Four times in the Epistle of 2 Peter, Yeshua is called "our Lord and Savior" (1:11; 2:20; 3:2, 18). And indeed, there are many other places in the Apostolic Scriptures where Yeshua the Messiah is unambiguously referred to as the Savior, including: John 4:42; Acts 5:31; 13:23; Ephesians 5:23; 2 Timothy 1:10; Titus 1:4; 2:13; 3:6; 1 John 4:14.

For some outsiders encountering the testimony of Scripture, there seems to be an issue. If the LORD God says that He is the only Savior and Redeemer of His people, then how can Yeshua the Messiah (Jesus Christ) also be referred to as the One who saves and redeems sinners? Is not this something that can only be done by God alone? The Biblical truth of the matter is that a human person being saved, forgiven of his or her sins, and being spiritually regenerated, **is directly connected to whether or not Yeshua the Messiah is Divine.**

We need to each consider the picture of the Ancient Israelites' Exodus from Egypt. Any one of us in the Messianic community, who has studied the Passover, should be fully aware of how the Passover lamb is a type and shadow of Messiah Yeshua (1 Corinthians 5:7), and that the Passover represents our exodus as Believers from slavery to sin to new life in Him.[2] The Passover is a picture of an individual's salvation. The Exodus account tells us that after the Lord had swallowed up the Egyptian armies that the Israelites began singing a song: "The LORD is my strength and song, and He has become my salvation; this is my God, and I will praise Him; My father's God, and I will extol Him" (Exodus 15:2). The Hebrew text says that *Yah v'yehi-li l'yeshuah* (וַיְהִי־לִי לִישׁוּעָה יָהּ), or "the LORD has become our *yeshuah.*"

This is not the only place where we see God as the *yeshuah* of His people. Psalm 118:14, 21 exclaims, "The LORD is my strength and song, and He has become my salvation [*l'yeshuah,* לִישׁוּעָה]…I shall give thanks to You, for You have answered me, and You have become my salvation [*l'yeshuah*]." Isaiah 12:2 says, "Behold, God is my salvation [*yeshuati,* יְשׁוּעָתִי], I will trust and not be afraid; for the Lord GOD is my strength and song, and He has become my salvation [*l'yeshuah*]." Perhaps most intriguing is Psalm 98:3: "He has remembered His lovingkindness and His faithfulness to the house of Israel; all the ends of the earth have seen the salvation of our God." This verse tells us that the world has seen *yeshuat Eloheinu* (יְשׁוּעַת אֱלֹהֵינוּ), in that the salvation of God is to have global ramifications. Such salvation extends far beyond physical deliverance from worldly trials and situations.

These verses from the Tanach affirm how God alone is the only Source of salvation, redemption, and deliverance from not

---

[2] Consult the author's article "The Message of Exodus."

only peril—but that He is the only steadfast One in whom people can trust and rely. God was the salvation for the Ancient Israelites, as the Supreme One removed them from their slavery in Egypt, being their salvation or *yeshuah*. If we are born again Believers, God has had to surely be *yeshuah* or salvation for us, leading us on an exodus out of the bondage we once had to sin and the forces of darkness, and into new life and restored communion with Him.

Is God our Savior? The conviction that Yeshua the Messiah must be Divine, God in the flesh, is deeply rooted in where the Source of one's salvation is found. The Source of our salvation is God Himself. God Himself is the only One who can save and redeem human beings from sin and the realm of death. The Psalmist expressed how, "No man can by any means redeem *his* brother or give to God a ransom for him—but God will redeem my soul from the power of Sheol, for He will receive me. Selah" (Psalm 49:7, 15). If Yeshua were only a human man or mortal, or even a created supernatural being, then could He legitimately have the power to deliver people from the clutches of death and eternal punishment (cf. Revelation 1:18)?

It is entirely appropriate for one to conclude that there is *no possible way* for Yeshua to be the Savior, providing eternal redemption for those who look to Him, unless He is truly God. Only if Yeshua is Divine, can He then be our Savior. The Hebrew Tanach is adamant about the LORD God being the only Savior, and if Yeshua is not the LORD God—a part of the Divine Identity—then who or what is He? How can Yeshua genuinely be the Source of eternal salvation if He is not God? Some have said that Yeshua only acts as "the Savior," meaning that He is God's agent in the world, but that He is ultimately not God. Yet, when we look at something as important as the intertextual quote of Isaiah 45:23 in Philippians 2:10,[3] it definitely forces us to acknowledge that Yeshua the Son is indeed the LORD (YHWH):

---

[3] Erwin Nestle and Kurt Aland, eds., *Novum Testamentum Graece, Nestle-Aland 27th Edition* (New York: American Bible Society, 1993), 518; Kurt Aland, et. al., *The Greek New Testament, Fourth Revised Edition* (Stuttgart: Deutche Bibelgesellschaft/United Bible Societies, 1998), 675.

"Declare and set forth *your case*; indeed, let them consult together. Who has announced this from of old? Who has long since declared it? Is it not I, the LORD? And there is no other God besides Me, a righteous God and a Savior; there is none except Me. Turn to Me and be saved, all the ends of the earth; for I am God, and there is no other. I have sworn by Myself, the word has gone forth from My mouth in righteousness and will not turn back, that to Me every knee will bow, every tongue will swear *allegiance*" (Isaiah 45:21-23).

"God highly exalted Him, and bestowed on Him the name which is above every name, so that at the name of Yeshua EVERY KNEE WILL BOW [Isaiah 45:23], of those who are in heaven and on earth and under the earth, and that every tongue will confess that Yeshua the Messiah is Lord, to the glory of God the Father" (Philippians 2:9-11).

The implications, of Isaiah 45:21-23 and Philippians 2:9-11 viewed together, are completely unavoidable. The One God of Israel, who has directly insisted that He is the only Savior to which all must turn for deliverance—who specifically says "there is no other[4]" (Isaiah 45:22)—has actually *shared* this status with Yeshua. This should not be surprising, as Yeshua is stated to be One "existing in the form of God" (Philippians 2:6, ASV). Not only is Yeshua the Messiah (Jesus Christ) the One to whom all of Creation and all created beings (human *and* supernatural) must give an account, confessing His supremacy and worshipping Him—but the Father and Son definitely co-exist as a part of a plural Godhead, with the Son having the same Divine Identity as His Father.

The statement of Isaiah 45:21-23 about God being the exclusive Savior to whom the whole Earth must turn and swear allegiance, and Yeshua being the One to whom every knee will likewise bow and every tongue confess—makes it definite "that Yeshua the Messiah is *ADONAI*" (CJB), and not a mere human master. A word like Isaiah 45:21-23 applied to any mere human agent empowered by God, or some supernatural yet created

---

[4] Heb. *v'ein od* (וְאֵין עוֹד).

agent, would immediately invoke an accusation of blasphemy, yet the *Carmen Christi* hymn of Philippians 2:5-11 is widely believed by conservative expositors to be a very early form of liturgy used by the Body of Messiah, representing a high Christology of Yeshua being Divine, which the Apostle Paul incorporated into his letter.[5]

Whether or not Yeshua the Messiah is God, **is indeed a salvation issue.** None of us as limited human beings may fully understand all of the complexities of Yeshua's Divinity, His pre-existence of Creation, and His co-existence with the Father—but we *must acknowledge* a Divine Redeemer in order to be forgiven of our sins and be saved from eternal punishment. We need to make sure that if we indeed must profess that Yeshua is Lord, it is those who have received the eternal redemption He offers—and not the condemned who will have to acknowledge Him at the Great White Throne judgment, before their final sentencing.

Answering these "Frequently Avoided Questions"

There are many claims that those who deny the Divinity of Yeshua, and thus deny the Biblical reality that we must have a Divine Savior, make, in saying that Yeshua is not God. Many of the arguments that anti-Divinity proponents make tend to be sensationalistic, and they can definitely prey on various individuals' unfamiliarity and/or ignorance of the Bible. Those who are undiscerning, and especially those who have perhaps not have had the spiritual encounter with the Creator through the Divine Messiah that they think they have had, are quite susceptible to these arguments.

It has become commonplace, when trying to challenge Yeshua as the Divine Messiah, to see various lists and compilations floating around, called something like the "Frequently Avoided Questions." Perhaps it is because these questions are so easily answered, that various Messianic Bible teachers who fully affirm Yeshua's Divinity, have not really taken the time to answer them. This analysis that I have provided

---

[5] For a further examination, consult the author's commentary *Philippians for the Practical Messianic.*

you is intended to address ten of these specific so-called "Frequently Avoided Questions," which are often used to claim that the Messiah is not Divine. You will find that these questions can be answered, that they are usually based on a selective reading of Scripture passages only at the surface level, and that when deeper readings of the text are conducted they fully affirm Yeshua's Divinity. Yet, it is these questions that can get even relatively mature and Biblically-rooted Believers, caught totally off guard.

False Claim #1
God cannot die. If Yeshua the Messiah is God, then how could He die on the cross?

On the surface, this first reason against believing that Yeshua the Messiah is God may seem to have some validity. If we suppose that God is an eternal and an immortal being, and that Yeshua the Messiah is God, then how could Yeshua be God if He died a human's death on the cross? If Yeshua the Messiah actually died, could this mean that He was just a normal human being like the rest of us?

The Apostle John attests in John 1:14, "the Word became flesh, and dwelt among us, and we saw His glory, glory as of the only begotten from the Father, full of grace and truth." His Gospel opens with the critical statement, "In the beginning was the Word, and the Word was with God, and the Word was God" (John 1:1). The Word we know to be the Messiah Yeshua. John plainly testified **"the Word was God."** Yeshua the Messiah "dwelt among us" or "made his dwelling among us" (NIV), the "us" obviously being humanity at large. John 1:14 says *sarx egeneto* (σὰρξ ἐγένετο), meaning that the Word "became flesh." The Hebrew word for "flesh" used in the Tanach is *basar* (בָּשָׂר), which relates to *"flesh for kindred, blood-relations," "all living beings,"* and *"mankind" (BDB).*[6] Its Greek equivalent is *sarx* (σάρξ), "the substance of the body" (*Vine*).[7]

---

[6] Francis Brown, S.R. Driver, and Charles A. Briggs, *Hebrew and English Lexicon of the Old Testament* (Oxford: Clarendon Press, 1979), 142.

[7] W.E. Vine, *Vine's Expository Dictionary of New Testament Words* (Nashville: Thomas Nelson, 1980), 242.

The Creator God manifesting himself as a human being is not something new. In Genesis 18:1-2, the Lord appears to Abraham not only in the form of a man, but in the form of three men:

"Now the LORD appeared to him by the oaks of Mamre, while he was sitting at the tent door in the heat of the day. When he lifted up his eyes and looked, behold, three men [*sheloshah anashim*, שְׁלֹשָׁה אֲנָשִׁים] were standing opposite him; and when he saw *them*, he ran from the tent door to meet them and bowed himself to the earth."

God being present in human flesh, in the midst of mortals, is nothing new as far as the narrative of Scripture is concerned. However, when Yeshua came to the Earth, He did empty Himself of the exalted glory that He had in Heaven. The Messiah "emptied Himself, taking the form of a bond-servant...being made in the likeness of men" (Philippians 2:6-7). Yeshua *en morphē Theou huparchōn* (ἐν μορφῇ θεοῦ ὑπάρχων), clearly "existing[8] in the form of God" (Philippians 2:6, TLV), exclusively, prior to His Incarnation. When Yeshua came to Earth, He was "born in human likeness" (Philippians 2:7, NRSV), *homoiōmati anthrōpōn* (ὁμοιώματι ἀνθρώπων).

Yeshua came to Earth not only as a human being, but specifically *morphēn doulou* (μορφὴν δούλου), "the form of a servant" (Philippians 2:7, RSV/ESV) or a "slave" (NRSV), so that He might be sacrificed for all our sins (Philippians 2:8). Yeshua was subject to many of the same things that all human beings are subject to (Hebrews 2:17-18). However, the testimony of the Gospels is clear that Yeshua maintained His authority as God, as the demons would immediately recognize who He was, and He commanded authority over illnesses, diseases, and the weather.

The argument that "God cannot die" is often delivered without any consideration of what happened at the crucifixion and subsequent death of Messiah Yeshua. The Word, who was God, became flesh. The Messiah lived on Planet Earth as a human man. Human flesh is subject to a human death. Yeshua

---

[8] *Huparchōn* (ὑπάρχων) is a present active participle, which while rendered with the English past tense "was" in some versions, really means "existing."

the Messiah was executed upon a Roman cross, bearing the sins of the world. **But this does not necessarily mean that Yeshua "died," and then for a time passed into total non-existence.**

Hebrews 5:7 notes how, "In the days of His flesh, He offered up both prayers and supplications with loud crying and tears to the One able to save Him from death, and He was heard because of His piety." This is obviously speaking about the Son's obedience to the Father, and should necessarily cause us to think about the prayers offered in the Garden of Gethsemane before His arrest (Matthew 26:36-45; Mark 13:32-42). This concerns a time period labeled *tais hēmerais tēs sarkos* (ταῖς ἡμέραις τῆς σαρκὸς) or "the days of His flesh," a time when Yeshua was subject to mortality.

When Yeshua died at Golgotha (Calvary), **it was the Lord's flesh that died.** The mortal frame that the Word had taken on had expired. But Yeshua the Messiah did not then pass into total non-existence.

The Apostle Peter describes, "For Messiah also died for sins once for all, *the* just for *the* unjust, so that He might bring us to God, having been put to death in the flesh, but made alive in the spirit; in which also He went and made proclamation to the spirits *now* in prison" (1 Peter 3:18-19). Peter says that Yeshua died for human sins, that He was put to death by the flesh or sinful human hands (*sarki*, σαρκὶ),[9] and that "going in to the spirits in prison, He then proclaimed" (LITV). Yeshua surely did not "preach the gospel"[10] to those spirits who were in prison from the time of Noah and the Flood (1 Peter 3:20). Yet, Yeshua would have had to actually have *gone somewhere* in order for this to have occurred, even if it were going via the Spirit to issue a proclamation to such spirits in prison, of His sacrifice and victory via final atonement for sin offered.

---

[9] This assumes that the dative (case indicating indirect object) *sarki* is instrumental.

[10] The verb appearing in 1 Peter 3:19 is *kērussō* (κηρύσσω) or "to proclaim"; if some form of gospel declaration were intended then the verb *euangelizomai* (εὐαγγελίζομαι), "to bring good news," i.e., to evangelize, would have been much clearer.

We know from the account of Lazarus and the rich man in Luke 16:19-31 that *Sheol* or *Hades*, the realm of the dead, was once divided into a compartment for the righteous and a compartment for the wicked.[11] When Yeshua died, His spirit or consciousness went to the Paradise side for the righteous, as He had plainly stated the following to the thief who was executed on the cross beside Him:

"And he was saying, 'Yeshua, remember me when You come in Your kingdom!' And He said to him, 'Truly I say to you, today you shall be with Me in Paradise'" (Luke 23:42-43).

Some who deny the Biblical reality of a temporary, disembodied afterlife say that the comma in English can be moved in this passage to read, "Truly I say to you today, you will be with Me in Paradise," but that is not what the source text reads at all. The Greek *sēmeron* (σήμερον) means "*today, this very day*" (*BDAG*).[12] Yeshua certainly did tell the repentant thief that both of them, *that day*, would be in Paradise—not that it would be an event to come sometime in the distant future. (The vast majority of usages of *sēmeron* in the Biblical text deal with events that occurred on the same day as "today.")[13] In order for them to be in Paradise, Yeshua would have had to continue to exist, even if it were in another dimension.

The claim that "God cannot die" used against Yeshua's Divinity is invalid when we understand that it was not Yeshua the person who died—but rather that it was the flesh, the physical mortal body of Yeshua, which died. When Yeshua was executed on the tree, He told the thief beside Him that they would both be in Paradise that very day. When Yeshua was in

---

[11] Josephus *Discourse to the Greeks Concerning Hades* 1, 4.

Also consult the FAQ entry on the TNN website, "Luke 16:19-31."

[12] Frederick William Danker, ed., et. al., *A Greek-English Lexicon of the New Testament and Other Early Christian Literature*, third edition (Chicago: University of Chicago Press, 2000), 921.

[13] "In Mt. 27:19 Pilate's wife has had a bad dream today; this is an omen for a decisive day, but the immediate sense is the ordinary one. The usual sense is also present in the petition of Mt. 6:11: believers ask today for their daily bread from God. Similarly in 16:3 the reference is to today's weather, in 21:28 the father asks his son to work today" (E. Fuchs, "*sēmeron*," in Geoffrey W. Bromiley, ed., *Theological Dictionary of the New Testament*, abridged [Grand Rapids: Eerdmans, 1985], 1025).

Paradise, the righteous side of *Sheol* or *Hades*, He made a proclamation to those spirits who were in the side of the unrighteous in prison in Hell. Yeshua as a spirit being, continued to exist after His flesh expired, and the testimony we see in the Apostolic Scriptures about Yeshua is that God did indeed take on human form. Later, we know that Yeshua was resurrected—"you will not abandon me to Sh'ol" (Acts 2:27, CJB),[14] being brought up from the abyss (Romans 10:7)—and it is in His resurrected body that the Son now sits at the right hand of the Father in Heaven.[15]

False Claim #2
God cannot be tempted. Yeshua the Messiah was tempted by Satan in the wilderness. How can Yeshua be God if He was tempted?

The claim that God cannot be tempted to sin is based on James 1:13: "Let no one say when he is tempted, 'I am being tempted by God'; for God cannot be tempted by evil, and He Himself does not tempt anyone." The logic that is used against Yeshua being God is that since He was tempted by Satan in the wilderness that He cannot be God. On the surface for some people, it would seem that since Yeshua was tempted that this must mean Yeshua cannot be God. Yet when a responsible Bible reader factors in only a few more Scripture passages, we see that the argument against Yeshua's Divinity of "God cannot be tempted," was produced by a very simplistic mind.

We definitely encounter in the Gospels, "Then Yeshua was led up by the Spirit into the wilderness to be tempted by the devil" (Matthew 4:1; cf. Mark 1:13; Luke 4:2). We see that Yeshua was tempted three times, and each time the Messiah responded with quotations from Tanach Scripture to Satan. A major temptation delivered by Satan to Yeshua appears when he said, "If You are the Son of God, throw Yourself down; for it is

---

[14] Cf. Psalm 16:8-11.

[15] It cannot go unnoticed that many of the people who deny Yeshua's Divinity also do not believe in an intermediate afterlife before the resurrection. The author has responded to many of the claims against a conscious, post-mortem afterlife in his article "To Be Absent from the Body."

written, 'HE WILL COMMAND HIS ANGELS CONCERNING YOU'; and 'ON *their* HANDS THEY WILL BEAR YOU UP, SO THAT YOU WILL NOT STRIKE YOUR FOOT AGAINST A STONE' [Psalm 91:11-12]" (Matthew 4:6; cf. Luke 4:9-11). To this temptation, Yeshua responded with, "On the other hand, it is written, 'YOU SHALL NOT PUT THE LORD YOUR GOD TO THE TEST' [Deuteronomy 6:16]" (Matthew 4:7; cf. Luke 4:12).

In responding to the Adversary's lure to Yeshua to cast Himself down, the Messiah quoted from the Torah in Deuteronomy 6:16: "You shall not put the LORD your God to the test, as you tested *Him* at Massah" (cf. Exodus 17:7). The Hebrew verb of interest here is *nasah* (נָסָה), appearing in the Piel stem (intensive action, active voice), and not only means "to **put someone to the test**," but can relate to how "men **'tempt'** God" (*HALOT*).[16] The KJV/NKJV does render Deuteronomy 6:16 with, "You shall not **tempt** the LORD your God." The Greek Septuagint translates the Hebrew verb *nasah* with *ekpeirazō* (ἐκπειράζω), which certainly appears in the quotation of Deuteronomy 6:16 in Matthew 4:7 and Luke 4:12, and which the RSV has rendered with, "You shall not **tempt** [*ekpeirazō*] the Lord your God." Both *nasah* and *ekpeirazō*, while variably rendered as either "test" or "tempt" in English Bibles, can both relate to human beings *tempting God.*

Psalm 78:41, 56 informs us how, "Again and again they tempted [*nasah*] God, and pained the Holy One of Israel...Yet they tempted [*nasah*] and rebelled against the Most High God and did not keep His testimonies." The testimony of the Tanach is certainly clear that people have tempted God. "Although people were forbidden from putting God to the test, they often did so" (*AMG*).[17] The very character of God, though, as an Eternal and Omniscient Being, prohibits Him from at all being influenced by any mortal testing or tempting of Him. People, even up until today, have challenged God with many absurd or even obscene statements along the lines of: *"If God exists, then I*

---

[16] Ludwig Koehler and Walter Baumgartner, eds., *The Hebrew & Aramaic Lexicon of the Old Testament*, 2 vols. (Leiden, the Netherlands: Brill, 2001), 1:702.

[17] Warren Baker and Eugene Carpenter, eds., *Complete Word Study Dictionary: Old Testament* (Chattanooga: AMG Publishers, 2003), 736.

demand that He...," insisting upon an immediate and often ridiculous action of Him.

If we follow the logic that God cannot be tempted, and because Yeshua was tempted by Satan in the wilderness that He cannot be God—then how is this to be consistently applied to the Tanach? The Hebrew Scriptures are clear that the Ancient Israelites *tempted God* in the wilderness. Because God was tempted by them, does that then make Him *anything less than God?* Is our Eternal Creator something less than a Supreme Being, because He has been tempted and tried throughout human history—especially by those who challenge His existence? **Of course not.**

The proper understanding about God being "tempted" is not the Father or the Son being placed in the position of being tempted, but rather that God cannot succumb to temptation. Because God is perfect, He always has the power to overcome temptation and will never fall prey to sin. As J.A. Motyer so correctly puts it, "There is nothing within his whole nature to which that or any other temptation could appeal, or which would respond to that or any other base suggestion."[18] Yeshua was tempted in the wilderness by Satan, but He overcame temptation, as it was not Yeshua's nature to give in. In telling Satan "You shall not tempt the Lord your God" (RSV), He was in essence declaring Himself to be God, as the action of temptation was prohibited to be directly issued toward God! Yeshua could just as well have rebuked Satan with a retort of not to stand against His Father's work or plan—but instead issued a word that he was prohibited from tempting God, definitively placing Himself as the Messiah on the Divine side of things.

What makes Yeshua God—different from us as human beings—is that Yeshua does not have the sin nature we inherited from Adam (cf. Romans 5:12). Being God in the flesh, Yeshua definitely had the power to overcome sin. He could not have been tempted to fall prey to any testing, and thus sin, as Satan tried to tempt Him in the wilderness.

---

[18] J.A. Motyer, *The Message of James* (Downers Grove, IL: InterVarsity, 1985), 51.

False Claim #3
The New Testament Scriptures always present a difference between the Messiah and God, proving that they are not one and the same. Because of the separation of the Messiah and God, how can He be God?

It is correct that within the Apostolic Scriptures or New Testament, we see a co-existence of the Father and the Son presented to us. Because there is a separation between the Father and the Son, does this all of a sudden mean that the Son is something less than God? It should be legitimately asked: How can Yeshua be the Son of God, if He does not have the distinct and specific nature of being "God" (cf. Philippians 2:6)? What do we do with statements appearing in the Apostolic Scriptures, where there is an intention for both the Father and the Son to be represented as "God"?

The Gospel of John opens with the classic statement, "In the beginning was the Word, and the Word was with God, and **the Word was God.** He was in the beginning with God" (John 1:1-2). John teaches that the Word, the Messiah Yeshua who took on human flesh (John 1:14), was God. Some have claimed that since the Greek clause *Theos ēn ho Logos* (θεὸς ἦν ὁ λόγος), "the Word was God," lacks the definite article *ho* (ὁ) with *Theos*, that it is something only akin to the Word or Yeshua being something supernatural, but not God. The New World Translation, produced by the Jehovah's Witnesses, notably rendered John 1:1 with "the Word was a god." Yet, were the definite article *ho* to appear, i.e., "the Word was *the* God," it would mean that the Word was all that exclusively composed God, such as "the Word was *the* Godhead."[19] If John 1:1 communicated "the Word was *the* God," then the preceding claim "the Word was with God," *ho Logos ēn pros ton Theon* (ὁ λόγος ἦν πρὸς τὸν θεόν), would be unsustainable. As Leon Morris directs us, "John is leaving open the possibility that there may be more to 'God' than the

---

[19] Cf. F.F. Bruce, *The Gospel of John* (Grand Rapids: Eerdmans, 1983), 31; D.A. Carson, *Pillar New Testament Commentary: The Gospel According to John* (Grand Rapids: Eerdmans, 1991), 117.

'Word.'"[20] The Word, Yeshua the Messiah, is indeed God. The Word is not, however, exclusively or entirely all that composes the Godhead.

The fact that the Godhead is plural, meaning that both the Father and Son are Divine, is evident to Bible readers all the way back in the Book of Genesis. The Lord said in Genesis 1:26, "Let Us make man in Our image, according to Our likeness; and let them rule over the fish of the sea and over the birds of the sky and over the cattle and over all the earth, and over every creeping thing that creeps on the earth." Some say that the "Us" referred to is not God, meaning that *Elohim* (אֱלֹהִים) is not to be regarded as plural, but rather the "Us" is God speaking to His celestial court. But Genesis 1:27 says that "in the image of God He created him." The "Us" referred to has to be *Elohim* or God, as human beings were created *b'tzelem Elohim* (בְּצֶלֶם אֱלֹהִים), not in the image of the angels or any of the other powers in Heaven. Ecclesiastes 12:1 notably admonishes, "Remember also thy Creators [Heb. *bor'ekha*, בּוֹרְאֶיךָ][21] in days of thy youth" (YLT). This verse attests to the plurality of God, as "All things came into being through Him [the Word], and apart from Him nothing came into being that has come into being" (John 1:3). It was not only God the Father, but also Yeshua the Son (Colossians 1:16-17; Hebrews 1:2-3), who is credited as being directly responsible for creating the universe (cf. Proverbs 30:4).

In the Apostolic Writings, when God is most often referred to, the reference made is to God the Father. This is because the Father is necessarily presented as greater than the Son, as the Son was sent by the Father into the world. In the Pauline letters, we see the greeting frequently issued, "Grace to you and peace from God our Father and the Lord Yeshua the Messiah" (Romans 1:7; 1 Corinthians 1:3; 2 Corinthians 1:2; Galatians 1:3; Ephesians 1:2; Philippians 1:2; Colossians 1:3; 1 Thessalonians 1:1; 2 Thessalonians 1:1; Philemon 3). Notice how "God" (*Theos*, θεός) is

---

[20] Leon Morris, *New International Commentary on the New Testament: The Gospel According to John* (Grand Rapids: Eerdmans, 1971), 78.

[21] The Hebrew *bor'ekha* (בּוֹרְאֶיךָ) is a plural Qal participle.

most always a title used in reference to the Father.[22] Notice also how with Yeshua the Messiah being called "Lord," that the title *Kurios* (κύριος) was used in the Greek Septuagint to render the Divine Name YHWH (יהוה),[23] and that with God the Father and Yeshua the Lord used in such close proximity, their association within the Godhead is unmistakably being referred to. Consider how Paul adapts the *Shema* of Deuteronomy 6:4 in 1 Corinthians 8:6, with the Father and the Son identified together: "for us there is *but* one God, the Father, from whom are all things and we *exist* for Him; and one Lord, Yeshua the Messiah, by whom are all things, and we *exist* through Him." Yeshua as Son (Lord) is integrated into the same Divine Identity as His Father (God).

Because "God" in the Apostolic Scriptures is most frequently identified with the Father, does not all of a sudden mean that Yeshua is not God. There are some places where Yeshua the Messiah is directly referred to with the title *Theos*. In Titus 2:13, Paul writes that Believers are to be "looking for the blessed hope and the appearing of the glory of our great God and Savior, Messiah Yeshua," identifying Yeshua as *tou megalou Theou* (τοῦ μεγάλου θεοῦ) or "our great God." Paul speaks of the Jewish ancestry of Yeshua in Romans 9:5, specifying, "from whom is the Messiah according to the flesh, who is over all, God blessed forever." The Epistle of 2 Peter is composed for "those who have received a faith of the same kind as ours, by the righteousness of our God and Savior, Yeshua the Messiah" (2 Peter 1:1). And surely not to be overlooked is how the disciple Thomas, upon seeing the resurrected Messiah, cried out to Him and exclaimed: "My Lord and my God!" (John 20:28). This was no mere statement of astonishment on Thomas' part, as he recognized Yeshua as being God, per Yeshua's own word of how "When you lift up the Son of Man, then you will know that I am [*egō eimi*, ἐγώ εἰμι]" (John 8:28a).

---

[22] Cf. D. Guthrie and R.P. Martin, "God: God as Father (2.2)," in Gerald F. Hawthorne, Ralph P. Martin, and Daniel G. Reid, eds., *Dictionary of Paul and His Letters* (Downers Grove, IL: InterVarsity, 1993), 357.

[23] Cf. L.W. Hurtado, "Lord: Appellation Formulas (3.3); Contexts (3.4)," in Ibid., pp 566-568.

In John 10:30, Yeshua told those assembled at the portico of Solomon, celebrating *Chanukah*, that "I and the Father are one." In oral Hebrew dialogue, He would have said something like *ani v'avi echad anachnu* (אֲנִי וְאָבִי אֶחָד אֲנַחְנוּ, Delitzsch) or *v'ani v'ha'av echad* (וַאֲנִי וְהָאָב אֶחָד, UBSHNT); the written Greek source text has *egō kai ho Patēr hen esmen* (ἐγὼ καὶ ὁ πατὴρ ἕν ἐσμεν). In using the word *echad* (אֶחָד) for "one,"[24] there is a correlation made with the *Shema* of Deuteronomy 6:4, "the LORD is one" or "The LORD is our God, the LORD alone" (NJPS). By Yeshua having said that He and the Father were one, He did not just claim that He and the Father were of one accord. Surely, many of the Jewish religious leaders of the day thought that they and God were of one heart and mind, in agreement and in one accord, in terms of how people were to live and conduct themselves. The reaction seen to Yeshua's claim that "I and the Father are one" (John 10:30) is, "The Jews picked up stones again to stone Him" (John 10:31).

The *Shema* is the declaration that only the LORD is the One True God. Did these Jews present pick up stones because Yeshua claimed that He was just in one accord with the Father? No. They picked up stones because in claiming that He was *echad* or one with the Father, they saw that Yeshua was claiming to be Divine, and they considered that to be blasphemous—*even with* Yeshua as the Son having noted that His Father is greater (John 10:29). Bruce Milne is right to note, "A claim such as this reflects no merely human consciousness. It is nothing other than a 'word made flesh' consciousness."[25] Earlier in John 5:18b, one of the reasons why the Jewish religious leaders are said to have wanted to kill Yeshua is because He "was calling God His own Father, making Himself equal with God."[26] They recognized that Yeshua

---

[24] If Yeshua were speaking Aramaic, then the closely related *chad* (חַד), as appearing the Peshitta New Testament, would have been used.

[25] Bruce Milne, *The Message of John* (Downers Grove, IL: InterVarsity, 1993), 154.

[26] The first reason stated in John 5:18a is, "He...was breaking the Sabbath." Here it is probably useful to keep in mind how the verb *luō* (λύω) can mean "*to loosen,* i.e. *weaken, relax*" (H.G. Liddell and R. Scott, *An Intermediate Greek-English Lexicon* [Oxford: Clarendon Press, 1994], 482), and Yeshua Himself gave the Disciples the authority to bind and loose (Matthew 18:18), meaning to consider proper application or *halachah* of various matters.

as the Son, presented Himself to them as having a very special relationship with His Father, and Yeshua was claiming to be of the same Divine substance as the Father. Yet as Philippians 2:6 explains, Yeshua "did not regard equality with God as something to be exploited" (NRSV) or "something to be used to his own advantage" (TNIV).[27] Yeshua the Messiah legitimately had equality with God, yet such equality could not be used by Him in order to avoid His humiliation and sacrifice for sinful humanity (Philippians 2:7-8).

There is a co-existence between the Father and the Son in the Apostolic Scriptures, but the Godhead has been plural ever since the beginning. References to "God" in the Apostolic Scriptures (particularly in the Pauline Epistles) are most often referring to God the Father. At the same time, Yeshua the Messiah is specifically referred to as "God" in various places as well. Most critical to recognize is that Yeshua is referred to as "Lord," and that "if you confess with your mouth Yeshua *as* Lord, and believe in your heart that God raised Him from the dead, you will be saved" (Romans 10:9). This is **not** just some recognition of Yeshua as "Master" or "Leader," for as C.E.B. Cranfield concludes, "The usage of κύριος [*Kurios*] more than six thousand times in the LXX to represent the Tetragrammaton [YHWH] must surely be regarded of decisive importance here."[28] This indeed indicates that acknowledging Yeshua the Messiah as God Incarnate, the LORD or YHWH, is required for salvation.

---

[27] While rendered elsewhere as "grasped" (2:6, RSV/NASU/NIV/ESV), the noun *harpagmos* (ἁρπαγμός) best means "**someth. to which one can claim or assert title by gripping or grasping,** *someth. claimed*" (*BDAG*, 133), often with some degree of violence or abuse.

[28] C.E.B. Cranfield, *International Critical Commentary: Romans 9-16* (London: T&T Clark, 1979), 529.

False Claim #4
To worship Yeshua as God is to worship another god. This is idolatry. How can you worship Yeshua as God? We are only supposed to honor or bow down to Yeshua.

The thrust of the First Commandment is quite clear in saying, "You shall not worship them or serve them; for I, the LORD your God, am a jealous God, visiting the iniquity of the fathers on the children, on the third and the fourth generations of those who hate Me" (Exodus 20:5; cf. Deuteronomy 5:9). This is a definite prohibition against idolatry, demanding that the LORD God of Israel be the only object of worship for the people, something repeated in any number of ways throughout the Torah.[29] In Exodus 20:5, the Lord instructs, *lo'tishtachaveh* (לֹא־תִשְׁתַּחֲוֶה), "You shall not worship," as this is something that is **to only be directed toward Him.** The specific verb that is actually employed here is *chavah* (חָוָה), which as *TWOT* informs us, appears "**exclusively in the Eshtaphal stem,** hishtaḥăwâ 'to prostrate oneself'; 'to worship.'" Its entry goes on and explains how in language studies, "Formerly this was analyzed as a Hithpael of shāḥâ [שָׁחָה] (q.v.). Cognate with the Ugaritic ḥwy 'to bow down' (UT 19:no. 847), used in parallel with kbd [כָּבֵד] 'to honor,' the verb occurs 170 times, in the majority of cases of the worship of God, gods, or idols" (*TWOT*).[30]

In the Greek Septuagint, Exodus 20:5 appears with, "Thou shalt not bow down to them, nor serve them; for I am the Lord thy God, a jealous God, recompensing the sins of the fathers upon the children, to the third and fourth generation to them that hate me" (LXE). The verb rendered as either "bow down" (LXE) or "do obeisance" (NETS) is *proskuneō* (προσκυνέω): "*to make obeisance* to the gods, *fall down and worship, to worship, adore*" (*LS*).[31] Obviously in the case of the First Commandment, *proskuneō* has to relate to worship.

---

[29] Exodus 23:24; Deuteronomy 4:9; 5:9; 6:13; 8:19; 11:16; 30:17.
[30] Edwin Yamauchi, "חָוָה," in *TWOT*, 1:267.
[31] *LS*, 693.

Worship of other gods, also involving some kind of bowing down or performing obeisance, or some other related devotion, is strictly prohibited in the Torah. For the Ancient Israelites, idolatry would not only merit capital punishment, but also incur reverberating curses being passed down to succeeding generations. So, if worship of Yeshua the Messiah is indeed idolatry, then many religious people—especially evangelical Christians who believe Jesus Christ to be Divine—have a significant degree of curses attached to them. Yet, if Yeshua the Messiah is genuinely Divine, being God, those who acknowledge Him as Savior are necessarily **required to worship Him.**

Various actions involving the verb *proskuneō* are witnessed in the Greek Apostolic Scriptures, in association with Yeshua the Messiah. A few of these actions do involve some kind of general honoring of Yeshua, but there are justifiable reasons to think of most of the places where *proskuneō* appears to regard actual worship of Him as Lord:

> "And when he [the Gerasene demoniac] saw Jesus from afar, he ran and **worshiped** [*proskuneō*] him; and crying out with a loud voice, he said, 'What have you to do with me, Jesus, Son of the Most High God? I adjure you by God, do not torment me'" (Mark 5:6-7, RSV).

> "Where is He who has been born King of the Jews? For we saw His star in the east and have come to **worship** [*proskuneō*] Him" (Matthew 2:2).

> "And he sent them to Bethlehem and said, 'Go and search carefully for the Child; and when you have found *Him*, report to me, so that I too may come and **worship** [*proskuneō*] Him'" (Matthew 2:8).

> "After coming into the house they saw the Child with Mary His mother; and they fell to the ground and **worshiped** [*proskuneō*] Him. Then, opening their treasures, they presented to Him gifts of gold, frankincense, and myrrh" (Matthew 2:11).

"When they got into the boat, the wind stopped. And those who were in the boat **worshiped** [*proskuneō*] Him, saying, 'You are certainly God's Son!'" (Matthew 14:32-33).

"And behold, Yeshua met them and greeted them. And they came up and took hold of His feet and **worshiped** [*proskuneō*] Him" (Matthew 28:9).

"When they saw Him, they **worshiped** [*proskuneō*] *Him*; but some were doubtful" (Matthew 28:17).

"And they, after **worshiping** [*proskuneō*] Him, returned to Jerusalem with great joy" (Luke 24:52).

"And he said, 'Lord, I believe.' And he **worshiped** [*proskuneō*] Him" (John 9:38).

Whether the verb *proskuneō* (προσκυνέω) is rendered as either "worship" or "bow down," in some of the notable passages appearing above from the Gospels, is undeniably something that is theologically motivated.[32] Is Yeshua the Messiah worthy of an

---

[32] Messianic Bible versions commonly encountered on the market today, and in various congregations, notably render the verb *proskuneō* in varied ways in these verses listed above.

The 1998 **Complete Jewish Bible** (CJB) has something along the lines of "fell on knees" or "fell down" or "prostrated" (Mark 5:6; Matthew 14:33; 28:9, 17; John 9:38), as well as the more customary "worship" (Matthew 2:2, 8, 11; Luke 24:52).

The 1998/2009 **ISR Scriptures** has something along the lines of "bowed down" (Mark 5:6; Matthew 14:33; 28:9, 17; Luke 24:52; John 9:38) or "do/did reverence" (Matthew 2:2, 8, 11).

The 2011 **The Messianic Writings** by Daniel Gruber employs "bowed down" (Mark 5:6; Matthew 2:11; 14:33; 28:9, 17; Luke 24:52; John 9:38) or "bow down" (Matthew 2:2, 8; 28:9).

The 2011 **Tree of Life Messianic Family Bible—New Covenant** (TLV) includes the renderings "bowed down" (Mark 5:6), as well as the more customary "worship" (Matthew 2:2, 8, 11; 14:33; 28:9, 17; Luke 24:52; John 9:38).

Of the four Messianic versions listed here, the TLV follows the exact same pattern as an evangelical Christian translation like the New American Standard (NASB/NASU), and would be the strongest in affirming worship of Yeshua with *proskuneō*. While David H. Stern's CJB might render *proskuneō* in some varied ways, Stern does affirm Yeshua's Divinity in his *Jewish New Testament Commentary*. As far as the Institute for Scripture Research or ISR is concerned, they have stated on their website (isr-messianic.org), "The ISR will not respond to doctrinal questions," and so there is no real way of knowing why certain things in the ISR Scriptures are

honor, which in the Torah is only to be given to God Himself? Of the examples listed above, the reaction of the demon-possessed man to Yeshua (Mark 5:6-7) and the Disciples on the Sea of Galilee when the storm was calmed (Matthew 14:32-33), probably immediately jump out at us the most. Are these just instances where various people bowed down or knelt to Yeshua as a sign of honor—or were they instances when the Divine authority that Yeshua exercised was acknowledged, and the people present knew that Yeshua was no ordinary human being?

There are a few places in the Gospels where the verb *proskuneō* appears, where worship of some kind is not really in view. Having to bow down may involve the physical condition of someone encountering Yeshua, or some kind of pleading. At least one example, that of the Roman soldiers taunting Yeshua, is a spiteful form of "worship":

> "They kept beating His head with a reed, and spitting on Him, and kneeling and **bowing** [*proskuneō*; mock worship, NLT] before Him" (Mark 15:19).

---

rendered the way they are. Some of the writings of the late ISR founder C.J. Koster lead one in the direction of thinking that the ISR Scriptures was not originally produced from a standpoint of Yeshua really being God/Elohim.

Also to keep in mind how there is no reference to any kind of worship directed toward Yeshua in the 2011 **Delitzsch Hebrew Gospels** (DHE) by First Fruits of Zion/Vine of David. The DHE has rendered the above verses from the Gospels with "bowed down" (Mark 5:6; Matthew 2:11; 14:33; 28:9; Luke 24:52; John 9:38) and "bow down" (Matthew 2:2, 8).

Obviously, the DHE is rendered from Franz Delitzsch's Hebrew translation of the Greek New Testament, where the verb *chavah* (חָוָה) was employed for *proskuneō* (προσκυνέω). All of the various forms of the verb *chavah* encountered in Delitzsch's Hebrew New Testament, also seen in the Tanach, have been rendered with "bowed down" in various mainline English versions. An exception to this to be taken into serious consideration, is where 1 Chronicles 16:29 says *hishtachavu l'ADONAI b'hadrat-qodesh* (הִשְׁתַּחֲווּ לַיהוָה בְּהַדְרַת־קֹדֶשׁ), "Worship the LORD in the splendor of holiness" (ESV). The Delitzsch version rendered *proskunēsantes* (προσκυνήσαντες) in Luke 24:52 as *hishtachavu-lo* (הִשְׁתַּחֲווּ־לוֹ), the same verb that appears in 1 Chronicles 16:29; Psalm 29:2; 96:9; 97:7 in regard to worshipping God.

The DHE lacks any explanation about why "bow/bowed down" was chosen in terms of reverent action directed toward Yeshua, and not the more customary "worship" as seen in more mainline versions. Perhaps in future editions some kind of statement can be made about this.

"And a leper came to Him and **bowed down** [*proskuneō*] before Him, and said, 'Lord, if You are willing, You can make me clean'" (Matthew 8:2).

"While He was saying these things to them, a *synagogue* official came and **bowed down** [*proskuneō*] before Him, and said, 'My daughter has just died; but come and lay Your hand on her, and she will live'" (Matthew 9:18).

"But she came and *began* to **bow down** [*proskuneō*] before Him, saying, 'Lord, help me!'" (Matthew 15:25).

"Then the mother of the sons of Zebedee came to Yeshua with her sons, **bowing down** [*proskuneō*] and making a request of Him" (Matthew 20:20).

In order to get a fuller picture of how the verb *proskuneō* is applied to Yeshua the Messiah, consider the following additional places where it appears in the Greek Apostolic Scriptures:

"And when He again brings the firstborn into the world, He says, 'AND LET ALL THE ANGELS OF GOD WORSHIP [*proskuneō*] HIM' [Psalm 97:7]" (Hebrews 1:6).

"And every created thing which is in heaven and on the earth and under the earth and on the sea, and all things in them, I heard saying, 'To Him who sits on the throne, and to the Lamb, *be* blessing and honor and glory and dominion forever and ever.' And the four living creatures kept saying, 'Amen.' And the elders fell down and worshiped [*proskuneō*]" (Revelation 5:13-14).

In Hebrews 1:6, we see a specific quotation made from Psalm 97:7, where it is asserted, "Let all those be ashamed who serve graven images, who boast themselves of idols; worship Him [*hishtachavu-lo*, הִשְׁתַּחֲווּ־לוֹ], all you gods." The Hebrew *kol-elohim* (כָּל־אֱלֹהִים) was rendered in the Septuagint as *hoi angeloi autou* (οἱ ἄγγελοι αὐτοῦ), in reference to God's angels, given some of the broad possible applications of the limited Hebrew term *elohim* (אֱלֹהִים).[33] The point made is that worship, which is directly intended for the LORD or YHWH (Psalm 97:5-6), **is here worship directed to Yeshua the Messiah.**[34] This is further intensified as Hebrews 1:8 informs us, "But of the Son *He says*, 'YOUR THRONE, O GOD, IS FOREVER AND EVER, AND THE RIGHTEOUS SCEPTER IS THE SCEPTER OF HIS KINGDOM' [Psalm 45:6]," with the Son clearly referred to as "God." Hebrews 1:10, also speaking of the Son, also says, "And, 'YOU, LORD, IN THE BEGINNING LAID THE FOUNDATION OF THE EARTH, AND THE HEAVENS ARE THE WORKS OF YOUR HANDS' [Psalm 102:25]," with the Son also referred to as "Lord." Both of these references should be recognized as affirming Yeshua as Divine.

Revelation 5:13-14 depicts John being shown the Throne of God, with the Father and the Son (the Lamb) seated together, and the elders issuing their worship. Worship of the Son does not negate worship of the Father.

While it would be linguistically valid to render the verb *proskuneō* as "bow down" or "kneel" in relation to action performed to Yeshua, whether or not it would be theologically valid can and should be legitimately challenged. In one's deliberations over whether or not Yeshua was actually "worshipped," one cannot deny when reverence or spiritual devotion was issued to Yeshua as depicted by the verb *proskuneō*, Yeshua did not make any effort to stop it. Contrary to this, there are some distinct places in the Greek Apostolic Scriptures where the verb *proskuneō* appears, of a human being performing action to either another human being or an angel, and the opposite party makes a decisive point to halt the action immediately:

> "When Peter entered, Cornelius met him, and fell at his feet and **worshiped** [*proskuneō*] *him*. But Peter raised him up, saying, 'Stand up; I too am *just* a man'" (Acts 10:25-26).

---

[33] Cf. *BDB*, pp 43-44.

[34] Among Messianic versions, the CJB and TLV have properly rendered *proskuneō* in Hebrews 1:6 with "worship." The ISR Scriptures 2009, while noting the quotation from Psalm (Tehellim) 97:7 in **bold text**, has "do reverence," although to be fair has rendered Psalm 97:7 itself with "Bow." The Messianic Writings by Gruber has "bow down" in Hebrews 1:6.

"Then he said to me, 'Write, "Blessed are those who are invited to the marriage supper of the Lamb."' And he said to me, 'These are true words of God.' Then I fell at his feet to **worship** [*proskuneō*] him. But he said to me, 'Do not do that; I am a fellow servant of yours and your brethren who hold the testimony of Yeshua; **worship** [*proskuneō*] God. For the testimony of Yeshua is the spirit of prophecy" (Revelation 19:9-10).

"I, John, am the one who heard and saw these things. And when I heard and saw, I fell down to **worship** [*proskuneō*] at the feet of the angel who showed me these things. But he said to me, 'Do not do that. I am a fellow servant of yours and of your brethren the prophets and of those who heed the words of this book. Worship God'" (Revelation 22:8-9).

The Apostolic Scriptures do demonstrate that Yeshua the Messiah was genuinely worshipped. In fact, the Father actually commanded it of His angels (Hebrews 1:6; cf. Psalm 97:7)— **meaning that worship of Yeshua is surely expected of human beings** as well. Yet, when a human being is witnessed to have attempted worship of either another human being or an angel, he is stopped from this action.

One common argument that will sometimes be made by those who deny that Yeshua the Messiah was worshipped as God, is that the verb *latreuō* (λατρεύω), "in the N. T. *to render religious service or homage, to worship*" (*Thayer*),[35] is not applied to Him. There is actually a very good reason why *latreuō* seldom appears in relationship to Yeshua the Messiah; it is because *latreuō* frequently renders the Hebrew verb *avad* (עָבַד), which itself tends to be associated with acts of cultic worship such as animal sacrifice and other physical acts in the Temple or Tabernacle. Yet, it would be impossible to claim that the Greek verb *latreuō*, with its Hebrew background via *avad* in view, is never applied to people serving Yeshua. The *TWOT* entry on *avad* informs us,

---

[35] Joseph H. Thayer, *Thayer's Greek-English Lexicon of the New Testament* (Peabody, MA: Hendrickson, 2003), 372.

"The...concept is used of serving Yahweh with the Levitical service (Num 3:7-8; Num 4:23, 30, 47; Num 8:11, 19 ff., latreuō for etc.). Interestingly enough, the LXX reserved the Greek word the official service of the priests only. The NT however, steadfastly resisted using this group of words for the NT ministry or its functions except in Rom 15:16, where it refers to Paul's labors for Jesus Christ. Instead, it reserved it for other religious contexts, especially those dealing with the OT ritual (Heb 9:21; Heb 10:11; Lk 1:23)."[36]

While it is not common for one to encounter the Greek verb *latreuō*, "serve," in association with devotion to Yeshua—precisely because of its close association with the Levitical priesthood and its sacrifices—it is nevertheless witnessed. The associated noun *leitourgos* (λειτουργός) is used by Paul in Romans 15:16, where he says he is "a minister of Messiah Yeshua to the Gentiles." It also has to be recognized that in some key Son of Man (cf. John 9:35-38; Revelation 1:12-18) passages in the Book of Daniel, that the Aramaic verb *pelach* (פְּלַח), "pay reverence to, serve (deity)" (*BDB*),[37] was rendered with *latreuō* in its Septuagint version:

"I kept looking in the night visions, and behold, with the clouds of heaven One like a Son of Man was coming, and He came up to the Ancient of Days and was presented before Him. And to Him was given dominion, glory and a kingdom, that all the peoples, nations and *men of every* language might **serve** [Ara. *pelach*; Grk. LXX *latreuō*; worshiped, NIV] Him. His dominion is an everlasting dominion which will not pass away; and His kingdom is one which will not be destroyed" (Daniel 7:13-14).

As Robert M. Bowman, Jr. and J. Ed Komoszewski explain in their book *Putting Jesus in His Place*, "the reference to all peoples 'serving' the Son of Man is confirmed as an expression of religious devotion. The One whom you may regard as the Ruler of your entire universe for all time is by definition your God, and it would be the height of folly *not* to render religious devotion or

---

[36] Walter C. Kaiser, "עָבַד," in *TWOT*, 2:639.

[37] Francis Brown, S.R. Driver, and Charles A. Briggs, *A Hebrew and English Lexicon of the Old Testament* (Oxford: Clarendon Press, 1979), 1108.

service to him."[38] So, while encountering the Greek verb *latreuō* in regard to Yeshua the Messiah is not common, the Son of Man, Yeshua the Messiah, who is granted the supreme authority by His Father, is indeed rendered worshipful "service."

If Yeshua is not God, then to worship Him would indeed be idolatry. However, the Apostolic Scriptures are clear that Yeshua was worshipped. When Believers today worship the Son, they do worship God—but never should worship of the Son at all subtract from worship of the Father. After all, in Philippians 2:11 we see "that every tongue will confess that Yeshua the Messiah is Lord, to the glory of God the Father." When people bend their knee and confess Yeshua the Son as Lord, the Father is glorified in all of it.[39]

False Claim #5
Yeshua the Messiah had to be born to exist. He did not exist until He was born. How can Yeshua be God if He had to be born to exist?

Those who deny Yeshua's Divinity have to dismiss any sort of concept of pre-existence, because Yeshua pre-existing the Creation of the universe lends undeniably strong support to Him being God. So, it is not uncommon for those who deny Yeshua's Divinity to barrage people with a statement like: "It is just common human sense that a person has to be born in order to exist." Yet, the full implications of the Messiah's emergence onto the scene of human history, from a Tanach prophecy such as Micah 5:2, have probably not been considered too deeply from those who deny Yeshua as God:

"But as for you, Bethlehem Ephrathah, *too* little to be among the clans of Judah, from you One will go forth for Me to be ruler in Israel. His goings forth are from long ago, **from the days of eternity** [*m'mei olam*, מִימֵי עוֹלָם]."

Did Yeshua the Messiah pre-exist His birth?

---

[38] Robert M. Bowman, Jr. and J. Ed Komoszewski, *Putting Jesus in His Place: The Case for the Deity of Christ* (Grand Rapids: Kregel, 2007), 69.

[39] For a worthwhile study examining the various worship and devotion issues surrounding Yeshua the Messiah, consult Larry W. Hurtado, *Lord Jesus Christ: Devotion to Jesus in Earliest Christianity* (Grand Rapids: Eerdmans, 2003).

The Gospel of John opens with a prologue very similar to the opening verses of the Book of Genesis. Just as Genesis 1:1 says, "In the beginning God created the heavens and the earth," John 1:1-3 says, "In the beginning was the Word, and the Word was with God, and the Word was God. He was in the beginning with God. All things came into being through Him, and apart from Him nothing came into being that has come into being." Further in John 1:14 we see that "the Word became flesh, and dwelt among us, and we saw His glory, glory as of the only begotten from the Father, full of grace and truth." The Word or *Logos* (λόγος)[40] is obviously a reference to Yeshua the Messiah. The affirmation of John 1:1-3 is that He was present at the Creation with God, **He was God,** and that all things were created by Him. John 1:1-3 certainly testifies that Yeshua pre-existed the creation of the universe as God, that He later took on human flesh, and that the Father and the Son co-exist as part of the Godhead.

In what is commonly called the *Carmen Christi* hymn of Philippians 2:5-11, its first statement about who Yeshua is, is that "He existed in the form of God" (Philippians 2:5). The clause *en morphē Theou huparchōn* (ἐν μορφῇ θεοῦ ὑπάρχων), is better rendered with "existing in the form of God" (HCSB/TLV), as *huparchōn* is a present active participle. Further on the statement is made that Yeshua "emptied himself, taking the form of a slave, being born in human likeness" (Philippians 2:7, NRSV). Just as Yeshua was existing in the form of God, further on Yeshua *morphēn doulou labōn, en homoiōmati anthrōpōn genomenos* (μορφὴν δούλου λαβών, ἐν ὁμοιώματι ἀνθρώπων γενόμενος). No reader would argue that *morphēn doulou* or the form of a slave/servant is anything but an authentic human-state for Yeshua to have. So, why would Yeshua existing in *morphē Theou* or the form of God be anything other than an authentic God-state? The hymn concludes with a direct appeal made to Isaiah 45:21-23 (Philippians 2:9-11), a Tanach passage where salvation is exclusively found in the LORD God, and all of Creation must

---

[40] Appearing with the *omicron* (o), the Greek term λόγος is properly pronounced with a short ŏ as *lŏgŏs*.

recognize His supremacy with no other. This is a status that Yeshua the Messiah, **as Lord,** has as well.

In the hymn of Colossians 1:15-20, the testimony given about Yeshua also affirms His pre-existence of the universe. "[F]or in him all things were created[41], in heaven and on earth, visible and invisible, whether thrones or dominions or principalities or authorities—all things were created through him and for him. He is before all things [exists before everything, TLV][42], and in him all things hold together" (Colossians 1:16-17, RSV). We may need to each be reminded of how God, and not only the Father but also the Son, being involved in the creation of the universe, is something clearly implied by Proverbs 30:4: "Who has ascended into heaven and descended? Who has gathered the wind in His fists? Who has wrapped the waters in His garment? Who has established all the ends of the earth? What is His name or His son's name? Surely you know!"

Some readers are caught a little off guard when they see the statement made that Yeshua is "the firstborn of all creation" (Colossians 1:15), and could be led into thinking that Yeshua had to be physically born to exist. Yet, anyone familiar with the Tanach should immediately note how the title "firstborn" (Heb. *bekor,* בְּכוֹר) is one of high, preeminent status. It is applied to people regardless of where or when they were "born," sometimes even if they were actually not the first born in their family line. Firstborn describes Reuben the son of Jacob (Genesis 49:3-4), the people of Israel as God's "son" (Exodus 4:22), King David (Psalm 89:27), and the Northern Kingdom of Israel/Ephraim (Jeremiah 31:9). The title "firstborn," possessing royal distinction, is appropriate for the King of Kings and His ultimate authority (Revelation 1:17-18). As it was said of King David, "I will make him the first-born, the highest of the kings of the earth[43]" (Psalm 89:27, RSV).

The designation of Yeshua as *prōtotokos pasēs ktiseōs* (πρωτότοκος πάσης κτίσεως) does not relate to a status of

---

[41] Grk. *hoti en autō ektisthē ta panta* (ὅτι ἐν αὐτῷ ἐκτίσθη τὰ πάντα).

[42] Grk. *estin pro pantōn* (ἐστιν πρὸ πάντων).

[43] Heb. *af-ani bekor et'neihu el'yon l'malkei-eretz* (בְּכוֹר אֶתְּנֵהוּ עֶלְיוֹן לְמַלְכֵי־אָרֶץ אַף־אָנִי).

possession—as though the Earth were to own Him as only being human—but instead relates to a status of preeminence. In the estimation of Daniel B. Wallace, the clause *prōtotokos pasēs ktiseōs* is a genitive (case indicating possession) of subordination, which would regard Yeshua's status as "the firstborn **over** all **creation**,"[44] the NIV/TNIV rendering. The title "firstborn" is one of great status and rulership, and if a reader can understand that **firstborn=anointed king** in Colossians 1:15, it becomes obvious that Yeshua is not a created being, and it is perfectly legitimate to treat *prōtotokos pasēs ktiseōs* as a genitive of subordination. Colossians 1:16-17, then, not only affirms Yeshua as the One who created the universe, but also that the universe was created for Him and it is sustained by Him. As Douglas J. Moo is right to conclude, "What holds the universe together is not an idea or a virtue, but a person: the resurrected Christ. Without him electrons with not continue to circle nuclei, gravity would cease to work, the planets would not stay in their orbits."[45] Concurrent with this, Yeshua's pre-existence of the universe and His presence in creating the universe—as well as His steady maintenance of it—is also affirmed in Hebrews 1:2-3:

"[I]n these last days has spoken to us in His Son, whom He appointed heir of all things, through whom also He made the world. And He is the radiance of His glory and the exact representation of His nature, and upholds all things by the word of His power. When He had made purification of sins, He sat down at the right hand of the Majesty on high" (Hebrews 1:2-3).

Surely also not to be overlooked, in terms of Yeshua's supremacy over all things—and indeed His pre-existence of the universe—is how Yeshua has the status of being "the first and the last." These affirmations appearing in the Book of Revelation, have an undeniable association with statements that the LORD

---

[44] Daniel B. Wallace, *Greek Grammar Beyond the Basics* (Grand Rapids: Zondervan, 1996), 104.

Other examples of a genitive of subordination provided by Wallace (Ibid., pp 103-104), include: Matthew 9:34; Mark 15:32; 2 Corinthians 4:4; 1 Timothy 1:17; Ephesians 2:2.

[45] Douglas J. Moo, *Pillar New Testament Commentary: The Letters to the Colossians and to Philemon* (Grand Rapids: Eerdmans, 2008), pp 125-126.

God makes of Himself in the Book of Isaiah, and how there is no other than He. Yeshua cannot be regarded as "the first and the last" unless He too pre-existed the universe *and* is God as well:

The First and the Last	
Book of Isaiah	Book of Revelation
"Who has performed and accomplished *it*, calling forth the generations from the beginning? 'I, the LORD, am the first, and with the last. I am He'" (Isaiah 41:4). "Thus says the LORD, the King of Israel and his Redeemer, the LORD of hosts: 'I am the first and I am the last, And there is no God besides Me'" (Isaiah 44:6). "Listen to Me, O Jacob, even Israel whom I called; I am He, I am the first, I am also the last. Surely My hand founded the earth, And My right hand spread out the heavens; When I call to them, they stand together" (Isaiah 48:12-13).	"'I am the Alpha and the Omega,' says the Lord God, 'who is and who was and who is to come, the Almighty'" (Revelation 1:8). "...And He placed His right hand on me, saying, 'Do not be afraid; I am the first and the last, and the living One; and I was dead, and behold, I am alive forevermore, and I have the keys of death and of Hades'" (Revelation 1:17-18). "Behold, I am coming quickly, and My reward *is* with Me, to render to every man according to what he has done. I am the Alpha and the Omega, the first and the last, the beginning and the end" (Revelation 22:12-13).

Yeshua the Messiah *did not* have to be born to exist, because there is ample testimony in the Apostolic Scriptures that He not only pre-existed the Creation of the universe—but that He indeed created the universe!

Yeshua the Messiah *did* have to be born to obtain human flesh, and as a result be sacrificed so that final atonement for human sin could be provided. Philippians 2:7-8 explains that Yeshua "emptied himself, taking the form of a slave, being born in human likeness. And being found in human form he humbled himself and became obedient to the point of death—even death on a cross" (NRSV). In Galatians 4:4-5 we see, "when the fullness of the time came, God sent forth His Son, born of a woman, born under the Law, so that He might redeem those who were under the Law, that we might receive the adoption as sons" (Galatians 4:4-5). Yeshua the Messiah was incarnated as a human being, born through a human woman and born under the Law, so that He might redeem those who were under the Law or subject to the Torah's condemnation and curse. As Romans 8:3 says, "For what the Law could not do, weak as it was through the flesh, God *did*: sending His own Son in the likeness of sinful flesh and *as an offering* for sin, He condemned sin in the flesh." Yeshua the Messiah entered into the world as a human being, to redeem fallen humanity from sin.

False Claim #6
The demons never confessed Yeshua to be God. How can Yeshua be God if the demons never confessed Him as such?

Does Yeshua's Divinity always have to be represented by people or supernatural entities specifically confessing Him to be "God"? Or, can *the actions* demonstrated toward Yeshua by people or supernatural entities—particularly in terms of worship and/or devotion—demonstrate Him to be God?

In Mark 5:1, Yeshua and His Disciples go to the territory of the Gerasenes, which was on the far eastern shore of the Sea of Galilee. This was an area heavily populated by pagans, where the people did not worship the God of Israel or follow the Torah. Mark 5:2-5 tells us, "When He got out of the boat, immediately a man from the tombs with an unclean spirit met Him, and he had his dwelling among the tombs. And no one was able to bind him anymore, even with a chain; because he had often been bound with shackles and chains, and the chains had been torn apart by him and the shackles broken in pieces, and no one was strong enough to subdue him. Constantly, night and day, he was screaming among the tombs and in the mountains, and gashing himself with stones." This man was so demon possessed, that he could not be restrained and chains could not even hold him down.

Immediately upon arriving on land, getting off the boat, this demon possessed man encounters Yeshua. We are told "Seeing Yeshua from a distance, he ran up and bowed down [*proskuneō*] before Him" (Mark 5:5-6). This man, being demon possessed, immediately recognized that there was something very unique about Yeshua. This is why the RSV more properly renders Mark 5:6 with, "And when he saw Jesus from afar, he ran and **worshiped** [*proskuneō*] him." The narrative continues, "What business do we have with each other, Yeshua, Son of the Most High God? I implore You by God, do not torment me!" (Mark 5:7).

William L. Lane describes how "the demon is fully aware of Jesus' divine origin and dignity. 'Son of the Most High God' is not a messianic designation but a divine one."[46] To this, James R. Edwards further explains, "The Greek verb for 'fell on his knees,' [NIV] *proskynein*, denotes prostrating oneself before a person to whom reverence or worship is due...When demoniac meets divine, it is a no-contest event."[47]

The demons, which possessed the Gerasene man, had no choice but to bow down and worship Yeshua as the Son of God. Not only this, but when inquired by the Lord as to who the demons' identity was, the response is "My name is Legion; for we are many" (Mark 5:9). By having implored the Messiah not to torment them (Mark 5:7), the demons surely recognized that He had the authority to issue final judgment against them.

The authority to issue final judgment against the wicked, be they either unrepentant human beings or the forces of darkness, **is something that only God Himself possesses.** Yeshua told the

---

[46] William L. Lane, *New International Commentary on the New Testament: The Gospel According to Mark* (Grand Rapids: Eerdmans, 1974), 183.

[47] James R. Edwards, *Pillar New Testament Commentary: The Gospel According to Mark* (Grand Rapids: Eerdmans, 2002), 156.

Apostle John in Revelation 1:17-18, "Do not be afraid; I am the first and the last, and the living One; and I was dead, and behold, I am alive forevermore, and I have the keys of death and of Hades." Yeshua is the One who has the supreme authority over the realm of death, and thusly who is to be judged and banished from the Kingdom for eternity. This is concurrent with how Yeshua is "the Alpha and the Omega" (Revelation 22:13), which is a title that is only given to the Lord God Himself (Revelation 1:8). Yeshua, because He is God, is the One who will issue the final judgment (Revelation 20:11-15).

False Claim #7
The Scriptures tell us that God is a spirit and that He cannot be seen. How can Yeshua be God if He could be seen by human people?

Yeshua the Messiah says in John 4:24 that "God is spirit, and those who worship Him must worship in spirit and truth." It could make sense on the surface, for some people to think that if God is indeed a spirit, that He cannot be seen by anyone. It is certainly true that God warns, "So watch yourselves, that you do not forget the covenant of the LORD your God which He made with you, and make for yourselves a graven image in the form of anything *against* which the LORD your God has commanded you" (Deuteronomy 4:22). The Ancient Israelites had left Egypt, and were entering into Canaan, both of them being lands where the people worshipped graven images as their gods. Israel was not to form graven images and worship them as "God." God was not to be contained to a gold or silver object, or a lump of carved rock. He is omniscient and omnipresent. Being a spirit, God is everywhere, and does not need to be restrained to one form or another.

In spite of God being a Spirit, the Apostle John attested, "No one has seen God at any time; the only begotten God who is in the bosom of the Father, He has explained *Him*" (John 1:18). If people saw the physical Yeshua, then the logic against His Divinity is that He cannot be God because God cannot be seen. But, never being able to see God *at all, ever*, could seriously contradict the plain reality that Moses saw the back of God and thus saw God, even if only in part: "Then I will take My hand away and you shall see My back, but My face shall not be seen" (Exodus 33:23). Moses is also attested to be the one "whom the LORD knew face to face" (Deuteronomy 34:10), *panim el-panim* (פָּנִים אֶל־פָּנִים). Abraham saw God in the form of three men (Genesis 18:2-3). God has shown Himself to people before, even with Him taking on human form. It would be best for us to understand no one ever seeing God, who is spirit, as a general statement for most people—at least up until the Incarnation of the Messiah.

John describes something very special in relation to Yeshua coming to the Earth. After saying that "No one has seen God," obviously meaning the Father, he then describes that people have surely seen "the only begotten God" (John 1:18). Here, Yeshua is specifically called, *monogenēs Theos* (μονογενὴς θεὸς).[48] The term *monogenēs* (μονογενής) **"pert. to being the only one of its kind or class, *unique (in kind)*"** (BDAG), which would surely relate to how Yeshua is "uniquely divine as God's son and transcending all others alleged to be gods" (BDAG).[49]

Why is Yeshua called **"the only begotten God"**? Yeshua is called "the only begotten God" because the Messiah is God in the flesh, as "the Word became flesh, and dwelt among us" (John 1:14). Yeshua the Son specifically came to Earth, so that we could all understand the Father. Yeshua was God in a human body, interacting with standard mortals.

---

[48] It is obvious that in some other Greek textual traditions, "The only begotten Son" (NKJV) or *ho monogenēs huios* (ὁ μονογενὴς υἱός), appears. Yet as Bruce, *John*, 45 observes,

"[W]hy would anyone think of adding *theos* to form the unique phrase *monogenēs theos* if the Evangelist had not written it so? If *monogenēs theos* is the original reading, then the Evangelist is repeating what he said of the Logos in the third clause of verse 1: since the Logos was God, the Only-begotten is God in that sense, for the Logos and the Only-begotten are identical."

The alteration of *theos* to *huios* by some copyists can be explained on the basis of wanting to conform to later appearance in John of "the only begotten Son" (i.e., John 3:16, 18). It is obviously the more difficult of the two readings to theologically contemplate, and a standard rule in textual criticism of the New Testament is that the harder reading is more likely the original one.

[49] *BDAG*, 658.

In the hymn of Colossians 1:15-20, which was likely composed to subvert some errant First Century ideas about the Messiah only being a kind of supernatural intermediary force[50]— but not Divine—Yeshua is called "the image of the invisible God" (Colossians 1:15), *eikōn tou Theou tou aoratou* (εἰκὼν τοῦ θεοῦ τοῦ ἀοράτου). Yeshua as the image of God is a concept seen elsewhere in the Apostolic Scriptures, specifically as He reflects the Father's glory (2 Corinthians 4:4; Hebrews 1:3). Yet in Colossians 1:15, Yeshua is described specifically as being "the image of the **invisible** God," meaning that He represents something that cannot be seen or is invisible, as the adjective *aoratos* (ἀόρατος) means *"unseen, not to be seen, invisible"* (*LS*).[51] Paul details how such invisibility is a quality that only God Himself possesses:

"Now to the King eternal, immortal, invisible [*aoratos*], the only God, *be* honor and glory forever and ever. Amen" (1 Timothy 1:17).

Given the preceding verses in 1 Timothy 1:14-16 which describe Yeshua the Messiah, it is proper to conclude that the designation of both *aoratos* and "the only God" applies to the Son, and not just the Father:

"[T]he grace of our Lord was more than abundant, with the faith and love which are *found* in Messiah Yeshua. It is a trustworthy statement, deserving full acceptance, that Messiah Yeshua came into the world to save sinners, among whom I am foremost *of all*. Yet for this reason I found mercy, so that in me as the foremost, Yeshua the Messiah might demonstrate His perfect patience as an example for those who would believe in Him for eternal life."

The "invisible attributes" are considered by Paul to be "His eternal power and divine nature" (Romans 1:20). If Yeshua is the "image of the invisible God"—and not just "the image of God"— what specific things would such invisibility relate to? Having taken on human flesh, what would the Messiah be able to reflect

---

[50] This is examined more fully in the author's commentary *Colossians and Philemon for the Practical Messianic*.

[51] *LS*, 86.

of His Father to the world of mortals? Ezekiel 1:26 gives us some important clues: "Now above the expanse that was over their heads there was something resembling a throne, like lapis lazuli in appearance; and on that which resembled a throne, high up, *was* a figure with the appearance of a man."

It can certainly be suggested that several of the Tanach's most significant theophanies involved pre-incarnate manifestations of Messiah Yeshua, as such an "image of the invisible God." The author of Hebrews speaks of how Moses "persevered because he saw him who is invisible" (Hebrews 11:27, NIV), a reference to the burning bush, which is notably preceded by a statement about his service for the Messiah (Hebrews 11:26).[52] Yeshua being the "image of the invisible God," should be taken as proof of His pre-existence.

With Yeshua having taken on human flesh in order for people to be reconciled to their Creator (Colossians 1:19-20), Paul can assert, "For in Him all the fullness of Deity dwells in bodily form" (Colossians 2:9). More to the point, *en autō katoikei pan to plērōma **tēs Theotētos** sōmatikōs* (ἐν αὐτῷ κατοικεῖ πᾶν τὸ πλήρωμα τῆς θεότητος σωματικῶς) includes the definite article: "For in Him all the fullness of **the Deity** dwells enbodied" (my translation). Yeshua is *the Deity* manifested in a body—and *the Deity* is everything that makes God out to be God![53]

---

[52] "[C]onsidering the reproach of Messiah greater riches than the treasures of Egypt; for he was looking to the reward" (Hebrews 11:26).

To this can be added 1 Corinthians 10:4, "and all drank the same spiritual drink, for they were drinking from a spiritual rock which followed them; and the rock was Messiah."

[53] The term *theotēs* (θεότης) is different than the more general term *theiotēs* (θειότης), often just meaning "Divinity." The term *theotēs* "occurs in the NT only in Col. 2:9. The one God to whom all deity belongs, has given this fullness of deity to the incarnate Christ" (E. Stauffer, "*theótēs*," in *TDNT*, 330). Contrary to this, *theiotēs* only regards how "something is divine, whether a god or imperial majesty" (H. Kleinknecht, "*theíotēs*," in Ibid., 331).

Among Messianic Bible versions, the TLV includes the accurate rendering "For all the fullness of Deity lives bodily in Him" for Colossians 2:9, which is unmistakenly similar to the NASB/NASU. The ISR Scriptures 1993/1998 has the rather puzzling, "Because in Him dwells all the completeness of the Mightiness bodily." The ISR Scriptures 2009, however, has made a slight improvement with, "Because in Him dwells all the completeness of Elohim-ness bodily."

God is a spirit and because God is a spirit we are prohibited in the Scriptures from making any representation of Him. But this does not negate the reality that God has manifested Himself in human form, as certainly attested by those same Scriptures.

False Claim #8
Psalm 110:1 is a proof text that Yeshua the Messiah is not God, and has been purposefully misrepresented by those trying to make the Messiah God. How can Yeshua be God when *adon* is a Hebrew title given only to human masters?

Psalm 110:1 is one of the most frequently quoted verses in the Tanach that is directly cited or referenced in the Apostolic Scriptures in relation to Yeshua the Messiah (Matthew 22:44; Mark 12:36; Luke 20:42-43; Acts 2:34-35; Hebrews 1:13). Yeshua quoted Psalm 110:1 in reference to the scribes' claim that He was only the son of David, and asked them why they called Him the son of David, when David called Him "Lord":

"And Yeshua *began* to say, as He taught in the temple, 'How *is it that* the scribes say that the Messiah is the son of David? David himself said in the Holy Spirit, "THE LORD SAID TO MY LORD, 'SIT AT MY RIGHT HAND, UNTIL I PUT YOUR ENEMIES BENEATH YOUR FEET.'" David himself calls Him "Lord"; so in what sense is He his son?' And the large crowd enjoyed listening to Him" (Mathew 22:41-46; cf. Mark 12:35-37; Luke 20:41-44).

The Apostle Peter quoted Psalm 110:1 in his proclamation that Yeshua was the Messiah at *Shavuot*/Pentecost, comparing the Messiah to David, and how David did not resurrect from the dead and subsequently ascend into Heaven as Yeshua did:

"For it was not David who ascended into heaven, but he himself says: 'THE LORD SAID TO MY LORD, 'SIT AT MY RIGHT HAND, UNTIL I MAKE YOUR ENEMIES A FOOTSTOOL FOR YOUR FEET'" (Acts 2:34-35).

When we examine how this verse is quoted by both Yeshua and His Disciples, it is done in the context of proving that the Messiah is more than just a normal human being than King David was, and that He has supreme power. Yeshua asked the scribes the question, "If David then calls Him 'Lord,' how is He his son?" (Matthew 22:45), telling them to look at the Messiah as far more than just the son of David and part of the Davidic line, but as the Supreme King. At *Shavuot*/Pentecost the Apostle Peter told those gathered that Yeshua had ascended into Heaven and was seated at the right hand of the Father. In Yeshua's own words before the Sanhedrin, Yeshua seated at the right hand of God was considered to be blasphemy, a definite proof of His Divinity:

"But Yeshua kept silent. And the high priest said to Him, 'I adjure You by the living God, that You tell us whether You are the Messiah, the Son of God.' Yeshua said to him, 'You have said it *yourself*; nevertheless I tell you, hereafter you will see THE SON OF MAN SITTING AT THE RIGHT HAND OF POWER, AND COMING ON THE CLOUDS OF HEAVEN' [Psalm 110:1; Daniel 7:13]. Then the high priest tore his robes and said, 'He has blasphemed! What further need do we have of witnesses? Behold, you have now heard the blasphemy'" (Matthew 26:63-65; cf. Mark 14:60-64; Luke 22:67-71).

The high priest considered Yeshua to be committing blasphemy because He said that He would be sitting at the right hand of His Father. Another instance where the Messiah was considered to be blaspheming occurs in John 10:32-33: "Yeshua answered them, 'I showed you many good works from the Father; for which of them are you stoning Me?' The Jews answered Him, 'For a good work we do not stone You, but for blasphemy; and because You, being a man, make Yourself out *to be* God.'" These Jews mentioned here considered Yeshua to be a blasphemer, because by performing various miracles He demonstrated His Divinity, and to them a Divine Messiah was apparently incompatible with their theology.

When we see how Psalm 110:1 is quoted in the Apostolic Scriptures, it obviously relates to the nature of Yeshua, as He demonstrates Himself to be Divine. But what about the Hebrew text of Psalm 110:1? Has it been "purposefully mistranslated" to prove the Divinity of Yeshua as some claim?

Psalm 110:1 reads **"The LORD says to my Lord: 'Sit at My right hand until I make Your enemies a footstool for Your feet.'"** Most Bibles render the Divine Name of God, YHWH, as "the LORD." In the Masoretic Hebrew text, this appears as *ne'um YHWH l'adoni* (נְאֻם יְהֹוָה לַאדֹנִי).[54] *TWOT* notes how "'*ādôn* usually refers to men," but it also states that "there are numerous passages, particularly in the Psalms, where these forms, which are the only ones to apply to men, refer to God."[55]

It is not inappropriate or manipulative at all to understand Psalm 110:1 as correctly reading *ne'um YHWH l'Adonai*. This is because the vowel markings underneath the Hebrew letters were not added to the Hebrew text **until the Seventh-Tenth Centuries C.E.** A commonly accessible resource to the layperson, like *Unger's Bible Handbook*, notes, "Before A.D. 500 Hebrew manuscripts had no system of vowel indication, except certain consonants to indicate long vowels. Between A.D. 600 and 950 Jewish scholars, called Masoretes (Traditionalists), invented a full system of vowels and accents to punctuate the text."[56] Without the vowel markings, the consonants that appear for the words *adoni* (אֲדֹנִי), which would be "lord" in the context of a human master, or *Adonai* (אֲדֹנָי), which would be "Lord" in the context of referring to God, appear **exactly the same** as *alef* (א), *dalet* (ד), *nun* (נ), and *yod* (י). As Michael Brown further explains,

"As every student of Hebrew knows, biblical Hebrew was written with consonants and 'vowel letters' only; the *vowel signs* were added hundreds of years later. Yet both '*adonai* (used only for Yahweh) and '*adoni* (used for men and angels...) are spelled identically in Hebrew, consisting of the four consonants '*-d-n-y*."[57]

Old Testament textual criticism has determined that the Masoretes, while eloquently preserving the Hebrew text of the Tanach since the compilation of the Masoretic Text in the Middle Ages, are likely to have made some alterations here or there. This is evidenced by the fact when some verses from the Tanach are

---

[54] *The Jerusalem Bible* (Jerusalem: Koren Publishers, 2000), 782.

[55] Robert L. Alden, "'*ādôn*," in *TWOT*, 1:12.

[56] Merrill F. Unger, *Unger's Bible Handbook* (Chicago: Moody Press, 1967), 883.

[57] Michael L. Brown, *Answering Jewish Objections to Jesus, Volume 2: Theological Objections* (Grand Rapids: Baker Books, 2000), 137.

Ibid., 138 goes on to further conclude, though, his view that "When Jesus quoted this verse in Hebrew, he would have said, *ne'um 'adonai la'adoni.*"

quoted in the Apostolic Scriptures (New Testament), they do not fully align with the Tanach. Often, these quotations do align with the Greek Septuagint, and the Hebrew text being referred to in the Tanach can align with the Septuagint if in some cases the vowel markings are changed. Readings among the Dead Sea Scrolls may also confirm that an LXX reading is superior to the MT, or that the Hebrew *Vorlage* behind the LXX is different than today's MT.[58] Areas of potential challenge are usually associated with Messianic prophecies, and it is for this reason why Christian Bibles do not exclusively use the Hebrew text for the Old Testament, and consult outside sources like the Greek Septuagint, Latin Vulgate, Dead Sea Scrolls, etc. Messianics today should learn to do the same.[59]

I am of the opinion that the Jewish scribes of the Middle Ages, who compiled the MT text widely used today, were likely to have known that Psalm 110:1 was a verse quoted in the "Christian New Testament" regarding the nature of Jesus. Could they have altered the vowel markings so that *a-d-n-y* (אדני) would read with *adoni*, a human master, rather than with *Adonai*, a clear reference to God? This is something to be considered in one's reading of the Tanach. Fortunately, we are aware of how when Psalm 110:1 is alluded to in a passages like Matthew 26:64; Mark 14:62; and Luke 22:69, that those hearing took notice of Yeshua's Divine status by it.

---

[58] Biblical references where the LXX and/or DSS may prove superior to the MT must all be considered on a case-by-case basis. The able interpreter must be acquainted with good, technical commentaries on various books of the Bible, which examine these issues in detail.

[59] We recommend that if you use a Hebrew text for the Tanach, that you have a critical text like the *Biblia Hebraica Stuttgartensia* (Stuttgart: Deutche Bibelgesellschaft, 1977). While this text reads practically identical to the Rabbinical Masoretic Text used in the Synagogue today, it does offer in its footnotes alternate readings that appear in the Greek Septuagint, Latin Vulgate, Aramaic Targums, Dead Sea Scrolls, and other ancient translations and Hebrew manuscript fragments.

Consult Emanuel Tov, *Textual Criticism of the Hebrew Bible* by (Minneapolis: Fortress Press, 2001), for a more detailed examination of the preservation and copying of the Hebrew Tanach.

False Claim #9
Yeshua the Messiah never said "I am God."
How can Yeshua be God if He never said "I am God"?

Those who do not believe that Yeshua is God, to some who encounter their arguments, and are shocked by them, can seem to have a case. There is no specific instance of the Messiah ever saying, "I am God." However, there are instances where He says "I am," and it is "I AM" of a very specific context. Interpreters across the spectrum have all had to recognize in their reading of the Gospels some specific places where Yeshua uses "I AM."

In the Hebrew Tanach when the Lord appeared to Moses at the burning bush, we see, "Then Moses said to God, 'Behold, I am going to the sons of Israel, and I will say to them, "The God of your fathers has sent me to you." Now they may say to me, "What is His name?" What shall I say to them?' God said to Moses, 'I AM WHO I AM'; and He said, 'Thus you shall say to the sons of Israel, 'I AM has sent me to you'" (Exodus 3:13-14). God specifically told Moses that He was to be identified as *ehyeh asher ehyeh* (אֶהְיֶה אֲשֶׁר אֶהְיֶה), "I Shall Be As I Shall Be" (ATS). It is from the Hebrew verb *hayah* (הָיָה) or "to be" that the Divine Name YHWH/YHVH (יהוה) is derived, a loose meaning of which would be something like "Eternal One." In the Greek Septuagint, the Hebrew phrase *ehyeh asher ehyeh* was rendered as *egō eimi ho ōn* (ἐγώ εἰμι ὁ ὤν), "I am THE BEING" (LXE) or "The One Who Is" (NETS).

Within the Tanach, it is the LORD or YHWH (Exodus 3:14; cf. Isaiah 41:4; 43:10; 46:4) who is the "I am," best identified with the Hebrew *ehyeh* (אֶהְיֶה) in Exodus 3:14: "I AM has sent me to you," *ehyeh shlachani eleiykhem* (אֶהְיֶה שְׁלָחַנִי אֲלֵיכֶם). Yeshua speaking *egō eimi* or "I AM," especially in some very distinct places, has long been recognized by numerous interpreters of the New Testament as an affirmation that the Messiah was identifying Himself as the One with supreme power. These include Yeshua's control over the weather, reactions to questions asked of Him, claims of salvation and redemption exclusively coming from Him, affirmations of pre-existence, and affirmations of His Messiahship. Yeshua's response to the Sanhedrin at His trial by speaking "I AM," is notably what ultimately convicted Him.

The following are some important places in the Gospels where "I AM" or *egō eimi* (ἐγώ εἰμι) appears in the source text, all of which have some significant degree of Christological importance:

"But seeing Him walking on the sea, they thought it to be a phantom. And they cried out. For all saw Him, and were troubled. And immediately He spoke to them and said to them, Have courage. **I AM** [*egō eimi*]! Do not fear" (Mark 6:49, LITV).

"But He kept silent and did not answer. Again the high priest was questioning Him, and saying to Him, 'Are You the Messiah, the Son of the Blessed *One*?' And Yeshua said, '**I am** [*egō eimi*]; and you shall see THE SON OF MAN SITTING AT THE RIGHT HAND OF POWER [Psalm 110:1], and COMING WITH THE CLOUDS OF HEAVEN' [Daniel 7:23]. Tearing his clothes, the high priest said, 'What further need do we have of witnesses? You have heard the blasphemy; how does it seem to you?' And they all condemned Him to be deserving of death" (Mark 14:61-64).

"And seeing Him walking on the sea, the disciples were troubled, saying, It is a phantom! And they cried out from the fear. But immediately Jesus spoke to them, saying, Be comforted! **I AM** [*egō eimi*]! Do not fear" (Matthew 14:26-27, LITV).

"But from now on THE SON OF MAN WILL BE SEATED AT THE RIGHT HAND of the power OF GOD' [Psalm 110:1]. And they all said, 'Are You the Son of God, then?' And He said to them, 'Yes, **I am** [*egō eimi*].' Then they said, 'What further need do we have of testimony? For we have heard it ourselves from His own mouth'" (Luke 22:69-71).

"See My hands and My feet, that **it is I Myself** [*egō eimi autos*, ἐγώ εἰμι αὐτός]; touch Me and see, for a spirit does not have flesh and bones as you see that I have'" (Luke 24:39).

"Jesus said to her, **I AM** [*egō eimi*]! the One speaking to you" (John 4:26, LITV).

"And the sea was aroused by a great wind blowing. Then having rowed about twenty five or thirty furlongs, they saw Jesus walking on the sea. And He having come near the boat, they were afraid. But He said to them, **I AM** [*egō eimi*]! Do not fear. Then they desired to take Him into the boat. And the boat was instantly at the land to which they were going" (John 6:18-21, LITV).

"Yeshua said to them, '**I am** [*egō eimi*] the bread of life; he who comes to Me will not hunger, and he who believes in Me will never thirst" (John 6:35).

"Therefore the Jews were grumbling about Him, because He said, '**I am** [*egō eimi*] the bread that came down out of heaven'" (John 6:41).

"**I am** [*egō eimi*] the bread of life" (John 6:48).

"**I am** [*egō eimi*] the living bread that came down out of heaven; if anyone eats of this bread, he will live forever; and the bread also which I will give for the life of the world is My flesh" (John 6:51).

"Then Yeshua again spoke to them, saying, '**I am** [*egō eimi*] the Light of the world; he who follows Me will not walk in the darkness, but will have the Light of life'" (John 8:12).

"**I am** [*egō eimi*] He who testifies about Myself, and the Father who sent Me testifies about Me" (John 8:18).

"Therefore, I said to you that you will die in your sins. For if you do not believe that **I AM** [*egō eimi*], you will die in your sins" (John 8:24, LITV).

"Then Jesus said to them, When you lift up the Son of Man, then you will know that **I AM** [*egō eimi*]; and from Myself I do nothing; but as My Father taught Me, these things I speak" (John 8:28, LITV).

"'Your father Abraham rejoiced to see My day, and he saw *it* and was glad.' So the Jews said to Him, 'You are not yet fifty years old, and have You seen Abraham?' Yeshua said to them, 'Truly, truly, I say to you, before Abraham was born, **I**

am [*egō eimi*].' Therefore they picked up stones to throw at Him, but Yeshua hid Himself and went out of the temple" (John 8:56-59).

"So Yeshua said to them again, 'Truly, truly, I say to you, I **am** [*egō eimi*] the door of the sheep'" (John 10:7).

"I **am** [*egō eimi*] the door; if anyone enters through Me, he will be saved, and will go in and out and find pasture" (John 10:9).

"I **am** [*egō eimi*] the good shepherd; the good shepherd lays down His life for the sheep" (John 10:11).

"I **am** [*egō eimi*] the good shepherd, and I know My own and My own know Me" (John 10:14).

"Yeshua said to her, 'I **am** [*egō eimi*] the resurrection and the life; he who believes in Me will live even if he dies" (John 11:25).

"From this time I tell you before it happens, that when it happens you may believe that I AM [*egō eimi*]" (John 13:19, LITV).

"Yeshua said to him, 'I **am** [*egō eimi*] the way, and the truth, and the life; no one comes to the Father but through Me'" (John 14:6).

"I **am** [*egō eimi*] the true vine, and My Father is the vinedresser" (John 15:1).

"I **am** [*egō eimi*] the vine, you are the branches; he who abides in Me and I in him, he bears much fruit, for apart from Me you can do nothing" (John 15:5).

"Yeshua, who knew everything that was going to happen to him, went out and asked them, 'Whom do you want?' 'Yeshua from Natzeret,' they answered. He said to them, 'I AM [*egō eimi*].' Also standing with them was Y'hudah, the one who was betraying him. When he said, 'I AM [*egō eimi*],' they went backward from him and fell to the ground. So he inquired of them once more, 'Whom do you want?' and they

said, 'Yeshua from Natzeret.' 'I told you, "**I AM** [*egō eimi*],"'"
answered Yeshua, 'so if I'm the one you want [so if you seek
Me, NASU], let these others go'" (John 18:4-8, CJB).[60]

Each one of these Gospel references, describing some aspect
of the ministry and service of Yeshua the Messiah, can be probed
for the significance of what *egō eimi* (ἐγώ εἰμι) or "I AM" involves,
where Yeshua likely orally spoke the Hebrew *ehyeh* (אֶהְיֶה) or "I
AM" as seen in Exodus 3:14. The direction of G.M. Burge cannot
be overlooked here, as he says, "In the many 'I AM' sayings Jesus
is publicly applying the divine name of God—and God's
authoritative presence, to himself. No prophet or priest in
Israelite history would ever have done this. For Judaism it is the
most severe christological affirmation of all, leading audiences in
the Gospel either to believe in Jesus or accuse him of
blasphemy."[61]

There are two important instances in the Gospels, where in
the narrative source text Yeshua speaks *egō eimi*. The first is at
His trial before the Sanhedrin (Mark 14:61-64; Luke 22:69-71).
The Messiah is asked, "Are You the Messiah, the Son of the
Blessed *One*?" (Mark 14:61) or "Are You the Son of God, then?"
(Luke 22:70). Yeshua replies with, "I AM," and there are quotes
made from both Psalm 110:1 and Daniel 7:23. In this instance,
Yeshua is ruled guilty of committing blasphemy, and is
condemned to death. Nothing could be clearer in that referring to
Himself with "I AM," that Yeshua was identifying Himself as
Deity. While there is no instance of Yeshua ever verbalizing the
Divine Name YHWH, per the practice in Second Temple Judaism
of the Divine Name only spoken on *Yom Kippur* by the high
priest (m.*Yoma* 6:2), Yeshua speaking "I AM" is about as close as
He ever got to speaking YHWH.

By the text employing *egō eimi*, Yeshua did *not* just say "I am
He," in the context of Yeshua being a human Messiah

---

[60] Other notable places where *egō eimi* is used include: Revelation 1:8, 17; 2:23;
21:6; 22:16.

[61] G.M. Burge, "'I am' Sayings," in Green, Joel B., Scot McKnight, and I.
Howard Marshall, eds., *Dictionary of Jesus and the Gospels* (Downers Grove, IL:
InterVarsity, 1992), 356.

empowered by God, as some might like to say. Ancient history proves that there were many people in the milieu of First Century Judaism who believed themselves to be the "messiah" or some kind of "savior" or "deliverer" for Israel (cf. Acts 5:36-37). But the difference between those others who believed themselves to be some sort of messiah, is that Yeshua said "I AM," and the testimony about Him is that He is God in human flesh. The Sanhedrin court considered this blasphemy, and Yeshua was condemned to be executed.

Note that Pontius Pilate asked, in regard to Yeshua's conviction, "Why, what evil has He done?" (Matthew 27:23). Yeshua did not break any Roman law. If He wanted to call Himself the Messiah, or even call Himself God, He could not have been convicted by Roman law unless He advocated an uprising against Caesar. Pontius Pilate did not care if Yeshua called Himself the Messiah, or God, or whatever. But the Sanhedrin condemned Yeshua because He claimed not only to be the Messiah, but to be the very God who identified Himself as the "I AM" before Moses at the burning bush. Pilate had to go along with what the Sanhedrin wanted in order to maintain civil peace.[62]

The second instance of importance regards a discussion that transpired between some Jews who are said to have believed in Yeshua about Abraham (John 8:31-47). Yeshua's teaching was certainly challenging their behavior and attitudes, and they refused to be convicted. These individuals considered Yeshua to be demon possessed (John 8:48-52), and they taunted Him by asking Him who He thought He was by making Himself greater than Abraham (John 8:53). Yeshua said that His glory comes from the Heavenly Father (John 8:54-55), and He then asserted, "Your father Abraham rejoiced to see My day, and he saw *it* and was glad" (John 8:56). Somehow, Yeshua had knowledge about what had transpired during Abraham's life on Earth, even though Abraham had been almost two millennia dead by this

---

[62] Consult the relevant sections of the author's article "The Last Seder and Yeshua's Passover Chronology."

time. The dialogue between Yeshua and these Jews then reveals something quite startling:

"So the Jews said to Him, 'You are not yet fifty years old, and have You seen Abraham?' Yeshua said to them, 'Truly, truly, I say to you, **before Abraham was born, I am.**' Therefore they picked up stones to throw at Him, but Yeshua hid Himself and went out of the temple" (John 8:57-59).

There is no escaping what the narrative text records with *prin Abraam genesthai egō eimi* (πρὶν Ἀβραὰμ γενέσθαι ἐγὼ εἰμί): "before Abraham was born, I am!" This is not only a definite statement of Yeshua's pre-existence, but also a statement of Yeshua's identification of being the "I AM," as the uncreated Son who has existed for eternity with the Father. The Jews present picked up stones because they considered Him to be blaspheming. Colin G. Kruse explains how "when Jesus said...'before Abraham was born, I am', he was identifying himself with God. Perhaps Jesus was also implying that Abraham, great though he was, had lived and died, but that he, Jesus, because he is one with God, remains forever as the 'I am'."[63] The view of David H. Stern in his *Jewish New Testament Commentary* is that "This [John 8:58] and 10:30 are Yeshua's clearest self-pronouncements of his divinity...It was very clear to the Judeans exactly what Yeshua's claim was, because they immediately took up stones to put him to death (v. 59) for blasphemy"[64] (cf. Leviticus 25:15-16; m.*Sanhedrin* 7:5).

In John 8:58, in saying "Before Avraham came into being, I AM!" (CJB), Yeshua affirms His pre-existence as God. **Yeshua did _not_ say,** "Before Abraham was born, I was" in the past tense.[65]

---

[63] Colin G. Kruse, *Tyndale New Testament Commentaries: John* (Grand Rapids: Eerdmans, 2003), 218.

[64] David H. Stern, *Jewish New Testament Commentary* (Clarksville, MD: Jewish New Testament Publications, 1992), 183.

[65] John 8:58 is a definite verse where Messianics need to be rather cautious with how they use the Delitzsch Hebrew New Testament Gospels by First Fruits of Zion/Vine of David. Here, Delitzsch's Hebrew New Testament has rendered the Greek *prin Abraam genesthai egō eimi* (πρὶν Ἀβραὰμ γενέσθαι ἐγὼ εἰμί), "Before Avraham came into being, I AM!" (CJB), as *b'terem heyot Avraham ani hayiti* (הֱיוֹת אַבְרָהָם אֲנִי הָיִיתִי בְּטֶרֶם), "before the existence of Avraham, I was" (DHE).

All Bible readers, Messianic and Christian alike, can have confidence that Yeshua the Messiah is God from the affirmations delivered to us in Scripture, which depict His power, authority, and pre-existence, where the source text employs *egō eimi* (ἐγώ εἰμι) or "I AM." The connection intended to be made is how the LORD or YHWH Himself once said, "I AM WHO I AM" (Exodus 3:14).

False Claim #10
God says that "I am not a man."

Bible readers cannot doubt the fact that Numbers 23:19a establishes that "God is not a man," *lo ish El* (לֹא אִישׁ אֵל). But can this be viewed as definitive evidence against the Eternal God taking on human flesh in the person of Yeshua the Messiah? No. Numbers 23:19b further explains *why* God is not a man, saying, "that He should lie, nor a son of man, that He should repent." The issue of Numbers 23:19 clearly relates to the incorruptible and unchanging character of God, as He follows through on His promises and commitments: "God is not man to be capricious, or mortal to change His mind. Would He speak and not act, promise and not fulfill?" (Numbers 23:19, NJPS). Human beings, most contrary to God, frequently say things that they do not mean, or commit to doing things that they either forget about or decide not to do.

The Qal perfect first person singular verb *hayiti* (הָיִיתִי) is certainly witnessed in the Hebrew Tanach. In Joshua 3:7 we see, "Now the LORD said to Joshua, 'This day I will begin to exalt you in the sight of all Israel, that they may know that just as I have been with Moses [*ki k'asher hayiti im-Moshe*, כִּי כַּאֲשֶׁר הָיִיתִי עִם-מֹשֶׁה], I will be with you.'" The DHE rendering of John 8:58 can certainly be used to affirm Yeshua's pre-existence of Abraham, but not necessarily Yeshua's identification with the LORD or YHWH.

While the Hebrew *ehyeh* (אֶהְיֶה) or "I AM" is seen in Exodus 3:14, and this was what we believe Yeshua orally spoke in the many places where the Greek *egō eimi* appears in the Gospels, the 1991 UBSHNT has rendered John 8:58 with *ani hu* (הוּא אֲנִי). This simple present tense Hebrew expression for "I am" appears in Isaiah 41:4; 43:10; 46:4 in reference to God, His supremacy, and His Deity. Why Delitzsch did not originally choose *ani hu*, which would have been far better than *hayiti* for his Hebrew New Testament translation, is probably unknowable, but is very problematic.

God is unchanging in His character, not only in His abilities to remain true to His Word and promises, but also in His righteous judgment. As we see in Hosea 11:8-9, "How can I give you up, O Ephraim? How can I surrender you, O Israel? How can I make you like Admah? How can I treat you like Zeboiim? My heart is turned over within Me, all My compassions are kindled. I will not execute My fierce anger; I will not destroy Ephraim again. For I am God and not man [*ki El anokhi v'lo-ish*, כִּי אֵל אָנֹכִי וְלֹא־אִישׁ], the Holy One in your midst, and I will not come in wrath." Human judges in executing punishment or chastisement can have a tendency to be unbalanced and unfair, exceeding what is most appropriate. In the case of the Lord, though, He knows the appropriate limits of judgment and punishment of His people.

The idea that a Bible reader can quote a half-verse from the Tanach or Old Testament, "God is not a man" or "God is not mortal," and from this assume that the Incarnation of Yeshua is invalid—is not only irresponsible, but is rather stupid at that. And why is this *stupid?* Is it not true that Psalm 14:1 and 53:1 say, "There is no God"? Of course these verses say *ein Elohim* (אֱלֹהִים אֵין). Does this not mean that there is no Eternal Creator at the helm of the universe? Does this not mean that human civilization is only the result of a distant cosmic accident? This is obviously where it is useful to keep in mind what Psalm 14:1 and 53:1 fully communicate:

> "For the choir director. *A Psalm* of David. The fool has said in his heart, 'There is no God.' They are corrupt, they have committed abominable deeds; there is no one who does good" (Psalm 14:1).

> "For the choir director; according to Mahalath. A Maskil of David. The fool has said in his heart, 'There is no God,' they are corrupt, and have committed abominable injustice; there is no one who does good" (Psalm 53:1).

The Tanach does say that "God is not a man," but this is a qualified statement regarding the character of God. With this in mind, we see in the words of Yeshua, "If you had known Me, you would have known My Father also" (John 14:7), as the Son surely represents the magnanimous character and moral incorruptibility of the Father as seen in passages like Numbers 23:19 and Hosea 11:8-9. Those who would offer the statement "God is not a man" as a proof against the Divinity of Yeshua, have not carefully read the surrounding text.

The Ongoing Issue of Yeshua's Divinity in the Messianic Movement

In the 1990s and 2000s, the issue of Messianic people denying Yeshua the Messiah as God was something often found out in the fringes of the Messianic world. It was something that many ministry and congregational leaders surely knew about, it was something that upset both them and their constituents, and it was something that was rightfully opposed. In the past, the issue of the nature of Yeshua, His pre-existence, His Divinity, and indeed His status as the LORD—remained in Messianic sectors not considered to really be a part of the mainstream. Now in the 2010s, however, all of the issues surrounding the Divine Identity of Yeshua the Messiah have steadily shifted toward the more mainline, recognizable Messianic sectors, organizations, and ministries. *Questions have been asked of some recognized leaders, and* ***not enough*** *have stepped up to directly affirm Yeshua as God.* No one is completely protected, today, from encountering someone in a position of Messianic leadership—who may not have completely Biblical views about the Divinity of Yeshua. Knowing who does, and who does not, believe that Yeshua is God in today's Messianic movement is something significantly blurred.

One very subtle trend, which has gone largely undetected by most in the more mainstream Messianic community, has been witnessed in seeing Yeshua the Messiah *exclusively* referred to as "the Master." Obviously within the Greek Apostolic Scriptures, Yeshua is referred to as *Despotēs* (δεσπότης), which in most English versions has been rendered as "Master."[66] The more prominent

---

[66] Cf. K.H. Rengstorf, *"despótēs,"* in *TDNT*, pp 145-146; M.W. Meyer, "Master," in Geoffrey W. Bromiley, ed. et. al., *International Standard Bible Encyclopedia*, 4 vols. (Grand Rapids: Eerdmans, 1988), 3:278.

and frequent title that Yeshua is referred to, though, is *Kurios* (κύριος). This is the same title that renders the Divine Name YHWH (יהוה) in the Greek Septuagint, with many taking it as a definite sign of His Divinity. While it is linguistically possible to render *kurios* as "master," why some people in the Messianic movement—who are notably not advocates of a Sacred Name Only perspective that treats the English title "Lord" with utter disdain[67]—would change English Bible quotes where Yeshua is called "Lord" to "Master," is that it could very well be with wanting to purposefully disconnect any association between the Lord Yeshua and the LORD God.[68]

There has been a proverbial "underground" of groups here and there, sitting in what many would consider "safe" Messianic congregations—which officially *and* rightfully affirm Yeshua as Divine—who do not believe that Yeshua is Divine. At the very most, they might consider Him to have pre-existed the universe as some kind of supernatural entity or force, but they would never consider Him to be the LORD or YHWH. *Their numbers are growing.* Their ability to spread their heretical beliefs and ideas is also increasing as well. The technological tools to spread information are making the job of congregational leaders and teachers, to protect people from false teachings against the Lord Yeshua, far more complex than they ever have been before.

What does this mean for the future? It means that we cannot be afraid or hesitant about speaking forth the truth of who Yeshua is as the Divine Savior. *Things are likely to get worse, and not better.* **Romans 10:9 is clear that this is a salvation issue, as Yeshua must be confessed to be the Lord (YHWH) in order for people to have eternal redemption!** While there are surely aspects of Yeshua's Divinity that limited humans cannot fully understand, and there are more studies and analyses to be conducted as one fine-tunes his or her understanding about Yeshua being both God and man—the Scriptures are clear that only a Divine Messiah can save us from our sins!

---

[67] This is analyzed further in the author's article, "Sacred Name Concerns."

[68] For some useful discussion, consult B. Witherington III, "Lord," in *Dictionary of Jesus and the Gospels*, pp 484-942; L.W. Hurtado, "Lord," in *Dictionary of Paul and His Letters*, pp 560-569.

This concludes our ministry response to the so-called "frequently avoided questions" relating to the Divinity of Yeshua. You have seen in our responses to the various questions posed, that arguments against the Divinity of our Savior are often surface level, they purposefully ignore other Scripture passages, and most of all they *ignore* the Biblical reality that only God and He alone can save us from our sins. Some ancient scribes recognized this in Yeshua when they asked, "Why does this man speak that way? He is blaspheming; who can forgive sins but God alone?" (Mark 2:7; cf. Luke 5:21). They believed Yeshua's forgiving people of their sins to be blasphemy because only God can forgive sins, as the Psalmist plainly declares, "Help us, O God of our salvation, for the glory of Your name; and deliver us and forgive our sins for Your name's sake" (Psalm 79:9).

If Yeshua the Messiah is not God, yet the Scriptures tell us that only God can save us from our sins and forgive us of our sins, then how can Yeshua be our Savior? If Yeshua is not God in the flesh, then who is He?

What are we to do about those who deny Yeshua as God in the flesh, yet still recognize Him as the Messiah? Have they left the faith? Thankfully, it is only up to the Lord of all to ultimately decide who is saved and unsaved, as only He knows the true heart intent of any individual. However, those who have denied Yeshua's Divinity have denied Him being a Divine Savior, and they have denied the Source of their salvation and the Biblical reality that only God can save us. **God help them all!**

The subject of Yeshua's Divinity is not going away anytime soon. There will be additional criticisms that will be given by those who are denying the Divine Savior, and this article will certainly not be the last piece written on the subject matter.[69] We need to be ready for what is coming—and hold on to the fact that He is the Divine Savior, because a human being cannot redeem another human being. We must always question the motives of

---

[69] The author is presently preparing a work, entitled *Salvation on the Line*, which will classify and examine all of the major passages, in detail, about the Divine nature of Yeshua from the Tanach and Apostolic Scriptures.

those who deny Yeshua's Divinity and His part as a member of the Godhead, wondering why they are doing what they are doing. It is the established pattern that once you deny Him as God in the flesh, it is not that much longer before you deny Him as the Messiah.

confronting issues

What Does the Shema Really Mean?

שְׁמַע יִשְׂרָאֵל יְהוָה אֱלֹהֵינוּ יְהוָה אֶחָד

Shema Yisrael, ADONAI Eloheinu, ADONAI echad

The *Shema* of Deuteronomy 6:4, **"Hear, O Israel! The LORD is our God, the LORD is one!"** represents for all Bible readers the most ancient creedal statement of belief. The *Shema* is repeated in the daily, traditional prayers of Judaism as found in the *siddur*, and it is certainly a major feature of synagogue worship on the Sabbath. Even in much of Christianity, the words of the *Shema* are repeated in prayer, song, and worship, as the primacy of the Supreme God over Creation is declared. For myself, I had to declare forth the *Shema* of Deuteronomy 6:4-5, along with Isaiah 6:1-2 and Ephesians 4:11-13, at my commencement ceremony when completing my M.A. in Biblical Studies at Asbury Theological Seminary.

When the *Shema* is invoked, there is intended to be a moment of extreme reverence issued for the God of Israel, as men and women are to focus on His holiness, His omnipotence, and what He requires of His followers. We are to all make sure that the Lord is the One to whom we direct all of our worship, adoration, and veneration—*and* that we obey His Word and heed His direction for our lives.

While the *Shema* of Deuteronomy 6:4-9 undoubtedly has an imperative for God's people of worshipping, loving, and serving Him—the *Shema* also has an important place in religious history as it concerns monotheism. When the Ancient Israelites left Egypt, and were preparing themselves to enter into the Promised Land, they would certainly need a "statement of belief," if you will, by which they would declare their exclusive loyalty to the LORD God, and not any of the other deities of Canaan. The *Shema* enjoined the requirements for God's commandments to be taught to the people of Israel, and that they were to instruct their children.

In much of religious studies since, and most especially today, approaches to the *Shema* have gone beyond what was originally intended for the Ancient Israelites. While all who profess the *Shema* claim that their devotion is directed to the God of Israel, there can be a wide difference of approach between how the *Shema* is viewed in Jewish theology and Christian theology—particularly when it comes to the statement "the LORD is one." In historical Judaism, the Lord being "one" means that God is a single entity. In historical Christianity, being "one" means that God is surely a prime entity, but that He may be composed of multiple elements like Father, Son, and Holy Spirit.

The debate, over whether God's oneness allows or disallows for a plurality of persons or manifestations, is one which has doubtlessly arisen within the broad Messianic movement. As with too many theological issues Messianics face, the subject matter of the *Shema* has become mired in some rather base human emotions and spiteful rhetoric, with not enough attention given to the Biblical text and the applications of the *Shema* that are encountered within the Scriptural narrative.

This article will analyze what is communicated by the *Shema* of Deuteronomy 6:4-9, the issue of oneness in the Bible and whether or not a plural Godhead is allowable, and some key applications of the *Shema* witnessed in the Apostolic Scriptures. This article will also consider the current approaches, both positive and negative, witnessed regarding the *Shema* in the Messianic community—and will provide some tentative conclusions on the historic Christian doctrine of the Trinity.

Deuteronomy 6:4-9
The Shema for Ancient Israel

"Hear, O Israel! The LORD is our God, the LORD is one!
You shall love the LORD your God with all your heart and
with all your soul and with all your might. These words,
which I am commanding you today, shall be on your heart.
You shall teach them diligently to your sons and shall talk
of them when you sit in your house and when you walk by
the way and when you lie down and when you rise up.
You shall bind them as a sign on your hand and they shall
be as frontals on your forehead. You shall write them on
the doorposts of your house and on your gates."

The *Shema* of Deuteronomy 6:4-9 is delivered after the Ten
Commandments have been repeated to the Ancient Israelites
(Deuteronomy 5:6-21). The close association with the *Shema* and
the Ten Commandments obviously makes what is to be declared
most imperative for the people. Within the Torah itself, the Book
of Deuteronomy or *Devarim* (דְּבָרִים), meaning "words," includes
a repetition of much of the Torah's previous instructions to
Israel. Our English term Deuteronomy is derived from its Greek
Septuagint designation of *Deuteronomium* (ΔΕΥΤΕΡΟΝΟΜΙΟΝ),
literally meaning "second law." This is taken from how a king of
Israel is told he "shall write for himself a copy of this law"
(Deuteronomy 17:18). The Hebrew of this is *mishneh ha'Torah*
(מִשְׁנֵה הַתּוֹרָה), as *mishneh* means "double, copy, second" (*BDB*).[1]
The LXX rendered this as *deuteronomion* (δευτερονόμιον). The
overall theme and message of the Book of Deuteronomy is that
the Ancient Israelites are to be prepared and readied to enter into
the Promised Land.[2]

That the word of Deuteronomy 6:4-9 is commonly called the
Shema is most obvious from its opening declaration: *shema Yisrael*
(שְׁמַע יִשְׂרָאֵל). In most Bibles this appears as "Hear O Israel!",
although the implication of the *Shema* goes well beyond people

---

[1] *BDB*, 1041.

[2] Consult the author's article "The Message of Deuteronomy," and the entry
for the Book of Deuteronomy appearing in his workbook *A Survey of the Tanach for
the Practical Messianic.*

audibly listening to a spoken word. Appearing in the Qal stem (simple action, active voice), the Hebrew verb *shama* (שָׁמַע) has a much wider variance of meanings than does the English "hear." *CHALOT* lists a number of possible usages for *shama* throughout the Hebrew Bible, including: "hear," "listen to," "heed," "hear=understand," and "be heard." *BDB* indicates that it can mean *"hear with attention, interest, listen to."*[3] The main purpose of the Israelites hearing what is stated in Deuteronomy 6:4-9, is not only that they might listen to the Instruction of God, but also that they would *act upon it.* The information contained in the *Shema* is not just a series of interesting facts and figures about God and what He expects of His people. Those who hear the *Shema* are to pay attention to its message, inculcate its words into their hearts and minds, and live accordingly in obedience. While considered a little antiquated, perhaps the rendering "Hearken O Israel!" better captures the idea of hearing, inculcating, and subsequently following what is stated in Deuteronomy 6:4-9.

The *Shema* requires five things to be followed by God's people:

1. To love God to the fullest, with all of one's being (Deuteronomy 6:5)
2. To take to heart the Word of God and His commandments (Deuteronomy 6:6)
3. To teach the Word of God, and speak about His commandments to one's children during daily affairs (Deuteronomy 6:7)
4. To bind the Word of God as a sign upon the arm and between the eyes (Deuteronomy 6:8)
5. To affix the Word of God to the doorposts of the house and upon the gates (Deuteronomy 6:9)

It is obvious, especially in the scope of Jewish interpretations of Deuteronomy 6:8-9, that these instructions were useful in developing the practice of binding *tefillin* (תְּפִלִּין) or phylacteries, and placing the *mezuzah* (מְזוּזָה) on one's doorframe. Some of these instructions have been viewed as being a bit symbolic by

---

[3] *BDB*, 1033.

various other readers, though.[4] The point to be taken, of course, is that no matter how the elongated *Shema* of Deuteronomy 6:4-9 is applied by those who hear it—is that God's Word, God's commandments, and God's activities in the lives of His people are to form their core identity. There is no specific detail regarding how God's Instruction or His Law is to be taught to people, just that it is to be taught and discussed—even at the family level. The *Shema* is not a place to debate the useful place of later Jewish synagogues, or any sort of religious academies of study. The *Shema* is to instead establish, in a very broad sense, the primacy of God's care for and involvement in the community of Israel. The *Shema* has theological and practical implications for how God is honored by His people.

What guides the *Shema*, more than anything else, is the requirement: "and you are to love ADONAI your God with all your heart, all your being and all your resources" (Deuteronomy 6:5, CJB), *v'ahavta et ADONAI Elohekha b'kol-l'vavkha u'v'kol-nafshekha u'v'kol-me'odekha* (וְאָהַבְתָּ אֵת יְהוָה אֱלֹהֶיךָ בְּכָל-לְבָבְךָ וּבְכָל-נַפְשְׁךָ וּבְכָל-מְאֹדֶךָ). Out of a love for God, then obedience to His commandments is to naturally come forth, which He is specific about when He states they are to "be on your heart" (Deuteronomy 6:5), *al-l'vavkha* (עַל-לְבָבֶךָ). Biblical history demonstrates that human beings trying to transcribe God's commandments on their own hearts—even with some useful methods of memorization and implementation possessing significant value—has ultimately been something lacking, as people still fall into various degrees of sinful behavior. This is why the impetus of the New Covenant is that God Himself would not only provide a permanent atonement for sin and forgiveness, but that His Spirit would supernaturally transcribe His Instruction onto the hearts and minds of His people (Jeremiah 31:31-34; Ezekiel 36:25-27).[5]

The practical importance of the *Shema*, for God's people, is to be manifested in how all actions performed in relation to Him result from love. This is why Yeshua the Messiah, in His

---

[4] Consult the FAQ on the TNN website, "*Tefillin*."

[5] Consult the author's article "What is the New Covenant?"

teachings to His followers, enjoined people to remember that the Deuteronomy 6:4-5 command is the foremost of all the Torah's commandments:

> "Yeshua answered, 'The foremost is, "HEAR, O ISRAEL! THE LORD OUR GOD IS ONE LORD; AND YOU SHALL LOVE THE LORD YOUR GOD WITH ALL YOUR HEART, AND WITH ALL YOUR SOUL, AND WITH ALL YOUR MIND, AND WITH ALL YOUR STRENGTH"'" (Mark 12:29-30).

> "'Teacher, which is the great commandment in the Law?' And He said to him, 'YOU SHALL LOVE THE LORD YOUR GOD WITH ALL YOUR HEART, AND WITH ALL YOUR SOUL, AND WITH ALL YOUR MIND.' This is the great and foremost commandment" (Matthew 22:36-38).[6]

Any and all proper handling of the *Shema* will recognize the centrality of God's place in the lives of His people, and how obedience to His Torah comes forth from the love that we are to have for Him. In the post-resurrection era of the New Covenant (cf. Hebrews 8:8-12; 10:16-17), where Yeshua the Messiah has been sacrificed for human sins, and permanent atonement and forgiveness have been provided—the Holy Spirit present within the lives of the redeemed is to surely compel them to live forth the essence of the *Shema!*

All readers of Deuteronomy 6:4-9 should be agreed that it enjoins God's people to love Him and obey Him, and it is not surprising at all why the word of Leviticus 19:18—"you shall love your neighbor as yourself"—is frequently associated with it.[7] What all readers of the *Shema* are not agreed upon is what the assertion in Deuteronomy 6:4, *ADONAI Eloheinu, ADONAI echad* (יְהוָה אֱלֹהֵינוּ יְהוָה אֶחָד), actually means.

In order for Messianic Believers to have an appropriate perspective on the *Shema*, we need to be able to understand what **"the LORD is one"** first communicated for the Ancient Israelites

---

[6] Cf. Luke 10:27-28.

Consult the useful discussion in the FAQ on the TNN website, "Leviticus 18:5."

[7] Cf. Mark 12:31; Luke 10:27.

in Deuteronomy. These were people who were being instructed by Moses for one last time, before Joshua would take over and lead them into the Land of Canaan. What would "the LORD is one" mean to them, set against an Ancient Near Eastern background of their immediate forbearers having been delivered from Egypt, and with them preparing to do battle—both physical *and* religious—with the Canaanites?

This is where it needs to be recognized that there is a wide array of interpreters, both Jewish and Christian, who rightfully acknowledge that the issue of *ADONAI Eloheinu, ADONAI echad* (יְהוָה אֱלֹהֵינוּ יְהוָה אֶחָד), as far as Deuteronomy 6:4 and its original purpose for the Israelites entering into the Promised Land was concerned—was not really the composition or makeup of God—but rather God's supremacy and primacy when set against the multiple gods of Canaan. The chart below has summarized a few opinions:

"the LORD is one"
JEWISH INTERPRETERS
"The Lord, Who is now only *our God* and not of other peoples, will in time to come be acknowledged by all the world as the one and only God."[8]   *Soncino Chumash*   "He is One, because there is no other God than He; but He is also One, because He is wholly unlike anything else in existence. He is therefore not only One, but the Sole and Unique God."[9]   J.H. Hertz   "At this stage in history, only Israel recognizes Hashem as One, thus He is *our God*; but in time to come, after the final Redemption, all the world will acknowledge that *HASHEM is One (Rashi)*....[T]he Torah says that Hashem is the *One and Only*—there is an inner harmony for all that He does, though human intelligence cannot comprehend what it is. This, too,

---

[8] A. Cohen, ed., *The Soncino Chumash* (Brooklyn: Soncino Press, 1983), 1022.

[9] J.H. Hertz, ed., *Pentateuch & Haftorahs* (London: Soncino, 1960), 770.

will be understood at the End of Days, when God's ways are illuminated."[10]
ArtScroll Chumash

CHRISTIAN INTERPRETERS

"[T]he passage is a confession set in opposition to the temptations of the Canaanite cult of Baal; in the other case it is a confession of the oneness of Yahweh in face of the multiplicity of divergent traditions and sanctuaries of Yahweh. Both interpretations can claim support from Deuteronomy."[11]
Gerhard Von Rad

"Yahweh was to be the sole object of Israel's worship, allegiance, and affection. The word 'one' or 'alone' implies monotheism, even if it does not state it with all the subtleties of theological formulation. Biblical monotheism was given a practical and existential expression which would lead to the abandonment of such views as monolatry. Even if some in Israel acknowledged the existence of other gods, the affirmation that Yahweh alone was Sovereign and the sole object of Israel's obedience sounded the death-knell to all views lesser than monotheism."[12]
J.A. Thompson

"These words, which have been called the fundamental monotheistic dogma of the OT, have both practical and theological implications. The Israelites had already discovered the practical implications when they celebrated the Exodus in song: 'Who is like you, O Lord, among the gods?' (Exod. 15:11), a rhetorical question inviting a negative response—there were no gods like the Lord! In the Exodus, the Israelites had discovered the uniqueness of their God and that the Egyptian 'gods' could do nothing to stop the Lord's people leaving Egypt. It was because they had experienced

---

[10] Nosson Scherman, ed., et. al., *The ArtScroll Chumash, Stone Edition*, 5th ed. (Brooklyn: Mesorah Publications, 2000), 973.

[11] Gerhard Von Rad, *Deuteronomy: A Commentary* (Philadelphia: Westminster Press, 1966), 63.

[12] J.A. Thompson, *Tyndale Old Testament Commentaries: Deuteronomy* (Downers Grove, IL: InterVarsity, 1974), pp 121-122.

> the living presence of their God in history that the Israelites could call the Lord *our God*. Thus the oneness and reality of the Lord were practical knowledge to the people."[13]
> Peter C. Craigie

The implication of *ADONAI Eloheinu, ADONAI echad* (יְהוָה אֶחָד יְהוָה אֱלֹהֵינוּ) in Deuteronomy 6:4, as recognized by an array of commentators, was to establish in the hearts and minds of the Ancient Israelites **the absolute primacy of their God.** In Craigie's estimation, "it is possible that 'one' is intended as name or title of God,"[14] with *echad* (אֶחָד) or "one" serving as a kind of status which His people would acknowledge of Him. It should not at all be surprising, then, why *ADONAI Eloheinu, ADONAI echad*—with *echad* relating to a status of being first—has passed into some Bible translations as "The LORD is our God, the LORD alone" (Deuteronomy 6:4, NRSV/NJPS) or "HASHEM is our God, HASHEM is the One and Only" (ATS). The *Shema* surely requires God's people to look to Him as their only Source of guidance, protection, and provision. God's people are to worship and venerate Him alone. And with this in mind, the *Shema* of Deuteronomy 6:4-9 would surely stand against any religious pluralism—because if the Lord is to be the sole focus of worship and devotion, then there are *not* multiple paths to the Supreme Being.

Does the Shema allow for a plural Godhead?

While it can be recognized that the *Shema* of Deuteronomy 6:4-9 was originally intended to assert the primacy of the LORD God of Israel as the sole Deity of worship and adoration for the Ancient Israelites preparing to enter Canaan—later theological and philosophical reflection upon the *Shema*, indicate that there has been application going beyond the original scope of the *Shema*'s intention. By the period of Second Temple Judaism, the declaration **"The LORD is our God, the LORD is one!"** became a

---

[13] Peter C. Craigie, *New International Commentary on the Old Testament: The Book of Deuteronomy* (Grand Rapids: Eerdmans, 1976), 169.

[14] Ibid., 168.

prime proof text for affirming Israel's monotheistic religion, especially set against a Greco-Roman world of polytheism, which was frequently trying to tempt Jewish people to embrace additional systems of worship (as most certainly indicated by the Maccabean crisis of the Second Century B.C.E.). Many liturgical prayers and praises issued to God, employed the *Shema* as some kind of a basis, and the *Shema* certainly affected the worldview of First Century Jews in terms of their interactions with others in the larger Mediterranean world.

The *Shema* of Deuteronomy 6:4-9 has been a place for considerable debate between both Jewish Rabbis and Christian theologians over the centuries, extending to the present day. Some of this has been colored by unfortunate anti-Semitic acts committed by various Christian religious and political authorities,[15] but much of it is also the result of different approaches to the text of Deuteronomy 6:4-9, and the relationship of the One God of Israel to Yeshua the Messiah (Jesus Christ). Does the statement of *ADONAI Eloheinu, ADONAI echad* (יְהוָה אֱלֹהֵינוּ יְהוָה אֶחָד) allow for a plural Godhead, with the oneness of *Elohim* (אֱלֹהִים) being a plurality? Most Jews will answer "No" to this, and most Christians will answer "Yes."

Among Jewish examiners, Richard Elliot Friedman, interpreting Deuteronomy 6:4, makes some appropriate observations in tune with the Ancient Near Eastern setting of the *Shema*. He states, "In comparing Israel's monotheism to pagan religion, we must appreciate that the difference between one and many is not the same sort of thing as the difference between two and three or between six and twenty. It is not numerical. It is a different concept of what a god is. A God who is outside of nature, known through acts in history, a creator, unseeable, without a mate, who makes legal covenants with humans, who is one, is a revolution in religious conception."[16] From this perspective, God being *echad* (אֶחָד) should be taken as an insistence upon God's grand uniqueness. The specialized

---

[15] Cf. Hertz, *Pentateuch & Haftorahs*, pp 920-924.

[16] Richard Elliot Friedman, *Commentary on the Torah* (New York: HarperCollins, 2001), 586.

challenge, of course, is recognizing that this God indeed does have multiple components to "Itself." Proverbs 30:4 asks the question, "Who has ascended heaven and come down? Who has gathered up the wind in the hollow of his hand? Who has wrapped the waters in his garment? Who has established all the extremities of the earth? What is his name or his son's name, if you know it?" (NJPS). When one sees the question *mah-sh'mo u'mah-shem-beno?* (מַה־שְּׁמוֹ וּמַה־שֶּׁם־בְּנוֹ), "What is His name or His son's name?" (NASU), that Yeshua as the Son of God can be integrated into the Godhead along with His Father, does find Tanach support. Those who affirm Yeshua's Messiahship, can also affirm some sort of special relationship that He has as a part of the Godhead as the Eternal Son.

So does "one," as it is used in key places in the Tanach and Apostolic Scriptures, allow for *Elohim* (אֱלֹהִים) or God to be a plurality?

"One" in the Hebrew Tanach

From the Creation account, it is often debated whether or not *Elohim* or God is an absolute one or a composite one. We read in the narrative, "Then God said, 'Let Us make man in Our image, according to Our likeness; and let them rule over the fish of the sea and over the birds of the sky and over the cattle and over all the earth, and over every creeping thing that creeps on the earth'" (Genesis 1:26). Christians have widely viewed this as a conversation that God is having with Himself, indicative of a plural Godhead. Jewish readers, in contrast, have largely interpreted the "Us" as a Heavenly court or celestial host, representing the Supreme Being and His angels. This second interpretation can run into a potential problem, as Genesis 1:27 further says, "God created man in His own image, in the image of God He created him; male and female He created them." The subject of this sentence is clearly *Elohim* or God, with human beings created *b'tzelem Elohim* (בְּצֶלֶם אֱלֹהִים) or in the image of God. Human beings were not made in the image of the angels, requiring that the "Us" of Genesis 1:26 to be God. From the very beginning of the Book of Genesis, clues are given to Bible readers regarding the plurality of God. It should not be taken as a coincidence that the most common Hebrew term for "God," *Elohim* (אֱלֹהִים), is the plural of *El* (אֵל).

As it relates to *ADONAI Eloheinu, ADONAI echad* (יְהוָה אֶחָד יְהוָה אֱלֹהֵינוּ) in Deuteronomy 6:4, there is considerable debate over what the word *echad* (אֶחָד) or "one" means. We previously discussed how among various examiners today, *echad* has been approached from the perspective of "The LORD is our God, the LORD alone" (Deuteronomy 6:4, NRSV/NJPS), which attests to the primacy of God in the lives of His people. It cannot go unnoticed, though, that Biblical Hebrew has several terms for "one." The Hebrew word used in the *Shema* of Deuteronomy 6:4 is *echad* (אֶחָד); it is to be differentiated from the word *yachid* (יָחִיד). Actual usage and context in various passages will obviously determine their proper meaning, but the Hebrew term *echad* (אֶחָד) can definitely have different connotation of "one" than *yachid* (יָחִיד).

A notable usage of ***echad*** appears in Genesis 2:24: "For this reason a man shall leave his father and his mother, and be joined to his wife; and they shall become **one flesh**." This speaks of a husband and wife becoming *basar echad* (בָּשָׂר אֶחָד) or "one flesh." This is two people, or two distinct entities, becoming one. In a proper marriage, there is a union between a man and a woman; they are one of purpose and one of substance, yet in being "one" there is co-existence of the two.

Echad representing the unity of a group of people is used in Genesis 11:6, speaking of humanity before the confusion of languages at the Tower of Babel: "The LORD said, 'Behold, they are **one people** [*am echad*, עַם אֶחָד], and they all have the same language[17]…'"[18] Later, in Numbers 14:15, the collective assembly of the Israelites is referred to as one man: "Now if You slay this

---

[17] Heb. *safah achat* (שָׂפָה אַחַת).

It cannot go unnoticed here how there is further flexibility in the Hebrew term *echad*, with it also meaning "**the same**" (William L. Holladay, ed., *A Concise Hebrew and Aramaic Lexicon of the Old Testament* [Leiden, the Netherlands: E.J. Brill, 1988], 133).

[18] Genesis 11:7 further says, "Come, let Us go down and there confuse their language, so that they will not understand one another's speech," which like Genesis 1:27 should be taken as a significant clue of God's plurality.

people as **one man** [*ish echad*, אִישׁ אֶחָד], then the nations who have heard of Your fame will say..." Both of these references, employing the Hebrew *echad*, are to composite groups of people as "one." When Americans recite the Pledge of Allegiance and say "one nation under God," they refer to a composite, united group, no different than what the Ancient Israelites were to be.

The most common usage that a reader of the Hebrew Bible, will actually encounter for the term *echad*, is in seeing it employed as a cardinal number—in the sense of #1, #2, #3, etc.[19] The term *echad* can also be used in an ordinal sense, representing "first," as in Genesis 8:13 it is used as a reference to the first of the month: "Now it came about in the six hundred and first year, **in the first** *month* [*b'echad l'chodesh*, בְּאֶחָד לַחֹדֶשׁ], on the first of the month, the water was dried up from the earth."

The Hebrew term *yachid* (יָחִיד), in contrast to *echad* (אֶחָד), is something that widely concerns "only, only one, solitary" (*BDB*),[20] and in some contexts can mean "**lonely, abandoned**" (*CHALOT*).[21] In Genesis 22:2, God tells Abraham to take his only son to be sacrificed: "He said, 'Take now your son, **your only son** [*et-binekha et-yechidekha*, אֶת־בִּנְךָ אֶת־יְחִידְךָ], whom you love, Isaac, and go to the land of Moriah, and offer him there as a burnt offering on one of the mountains of which I will tell you.'" This is representative of the fact that Isaac, and he alone, was the only son of promise given to Abraham. Later in Psalm 68:6, *yachid* is used to refer to the solitary: "God makes a home for the **lonely** [desolate, RSV; *yechidim*, יְחִידִים]; He leads out the prisoners into prosperity, only the rebellious dwell in a parched land."

Can *ADONAI Eloheinu, ADONAI echad* (יְהוָה אֱלֹהֵינוּ יְהוָה אֶחָד) be compatible with the concept that *Elohim* or God is a plurality of persons or manifestations? It is witnessed within the Hebrew Tanach that there are examples of *echad* or "one" representing a collection of multiple entities, and that the "oneness" present is a composite oneness and not an absolute oneness. It has been the

[19] C.L. Seow, *A Grammar for Biblical Hebrew*, revised edition (Nashville: Abingdon, 1995), pp 268-269; Bill T. Arnold and John H. Choi, *A Guide to Biblical Hebrew Syntax* (New York: Cambridge University Press, 2003), pp 32-35.

[20] *BDB*, 402.

[21] *CHALOT*, 133.

conclusion of many Christian interpreters, who affirm the Apostolic Scriptures' claim that Yeshua the Messiah is indeed the LORD God made manifest in the flesh, that the *Shema* allows for a oneness of *Elohim* of multiple components or manifestations. Such co-existent persons or manifestations would, at the very least, have to involve the Father and the Son.

Originally to the Ancient Israelites, the statement "the LORD is one" would have regarded the primacy of the Lord in the hearts and minds of the people as they were preparing to enter into Canaan. But, we cannot deny that implanted within the assertion *ADONAI Eloheinu, ADONAI echad* (יְהוָה אֱלֹהֵינוּ יְהוָה אֶחָד), is the claim that the Godhead is plural—otherwise readers should expect to have seen *yachid* (יָחִיד) used in the *Shema* of Deuteronomy 6:4 and not *echad* (אֶחָד). TWOT describes how "In the famous Shema of Deut. 6:4...the question of diversity within unity has theological implications. Some scholars have felt that, though 'one' is singular, the usage of the word allows for the doctrine of the Trinity [of Father, Son, and Holy Spirit united]. While it is true that this doctrine is foreshadowed in the OT, the verse concentrates on the fact that there is one God and that Israel owes its exclusive loyalty to him."[22] The statement that *Elohim* is *echad*, does very much seem to allow for a plural Godhead—similar to how husband and wife are to be "one flesh," or humanity at large is to be considered "one people." This conclusion, of *Elohim* being a composite oneness and ***not*** an absolute oneness, is not one that has been present in most of historical Judaism.

Earl S. Kalland explains some of the differences between Jewish and Christian approaches to *ADONAI Eloheinu, ADONAI echad* (יְהוָה אֱלֹהֵינוּ יְהוָה אֶחָד) in Deuteronomy 6:4. In the event that some of you have never seen the differences of approach, this summary should prove to be a bit useful:

> "To the Jews v.4 is not only an assertion of monotheism, it is also an assertion of the numerical oneness of God contradictory to the Christian doctrine of the Trinity of the

---

[22] Herbert Wolf, "אחד," in *TWOT*, 1:30.

Godhead. This kind of oneness, however, runs contrary to the use of אֶחָד ('eḥāḏ) in the sense of a unity made up of several parts. In Exod 26:6, 11, the fifty gold clasps are used to hold the curtains together so that the tent would be a unit ('eḥāḏ). Ezekiel said that the Lord directed him to join two sticks to represent Judah and Ephraim, for he was going to make the two kingdoms one, i.e., a single nation made of two parts (Ezek 37:17, 19, 22). This Jewish view of oneness also contradicts those statements in Scripture that show that God is Father, Son, and Holy Spirit. The verse declares the unity of the Godhead, viz., one God in three persons — though the Trinity of the Godhead is not [explicitly] taught in this passage."[23]

Obviously, the historic Christian doctrine of the Trinity, developed much later than the original giving of the *Shema* to the Ancient Israelites preparing to enter into the Promised Land. And, such a doctrine would certainly claim evidence from testimonies of God's composition that are witnessed in the Apostolic Scriptures or New Testament, in support of a plural Godhead. Yet, it can be affirmed that the *Shema* of Deuteronomy 6:4, with *Elohim* being *echad* or a composite one, laid the groundwork for later specification on what such a composite oneness of a plural Godhead would involve.

A common refutation, given against the plurality of the Godhead, is sometimes directed from Zechariah 14:9. It is prophesied that in the Last Days, "the LORD will become king over all the earth; on that day the LORD will be one and his name one" (RSV). We are told *b'yom ha'hu yiyeh ADONAI echad u'sh'mo echad* (בַּיּוֹם הַהוּא יִהְיֶה יְהוָה אֶחָד וּשְׁמוֹ אֶחָד). This is actually an important place where the Hebrew *echad*, relating to primacy, is doubtlessly in view. The LORD God of Israel will be the only Deity that all of humankind will look to when His Kingdom comes to Earth, as Zechariah 13:2 has previously stated, "'It will come about in that day,' declares the LORD of hosts, 'that I will cut off the names of the idols from the land, and they will no longer be remembered; and I will also remove the prophets and

---

[23] Earl S. Kalland, "Deuteronomy," in Frank E. Gaebelein, ed. et. al., *Expositor's Bible Commentary* (Grand Rapids: Zondervan, 1992), 2:65.

the unclean spirit from the land.'" Commenting on Deuteronomy 6:4; Zechariah 13:12; 14:9, Jewish commentator Jeffrey H. Tigay observes, "Deuteronomy and Zechariah both use 'one' in the sense of 'alone,' 'exclusively.'"[24] In his estimation, this will mean "that for all of humanity, YHVH and His name will stand alone, unrivaled....YHVH will be recognized exclusively and His name alone will be invoked in prayer and oaths."[25]

Opponents of a plural Godhead claim that since God's name will be "one," that this cannot possibly be representative of a plurality of *Elohim*. But in recognizing that *echad* (אֶחָד) has a wider array of applications than does the English #1, we can understand what this text is really saying. Michael Brown rightly concludes that this "is a prophecy of all peoples turning to Yahweh, forsaking their idols and false religions and worshipping him alone. It tells us nothing about the nature of his oneness. All it says is that he, the one true God, will be worshipped by all."[26]

In the Hebrew Tanach, *echad* (אֶחָד) has the dual meaning of both representing "one" in a composite sense, and representing "one" in a primary sense. Our God is "one" in that He is to be primary in our lives. Our God is one in that He manifests Himself by a plurality of entities (i.e., the Father, Son, and Holy Spirit), but yet these components of the Godhead are all unified similar to how a husband and wife are "one flesh."

If the *Shema* of Deuteronomy 6:4 were truly speaking of *Elohim* or God as an absolute unity of a single person or entity, then the word *yachid* (יָחִיד) would have been used, instead of *echad*, for "one." Interestingly enough, as Brown informs us, this "idea [was] expressed most clearly in the twelfth century by Moses Maimonides, who asserted that the Jewish people must believe that God is *yachid*, an 'only' one...the view of Maimonides is reactionary and also goes beyond what is stated in the Scriptures."[27] The Hebrew Tanach, though, does not say

---

[24] Jeffrey H. Tigay, *JPS Torah Commentary: Deuteronomy* (Philadelphia: Jewish Publication Society, 1996), 76.

[25] Ibid.

[26] Brown, *Answering Jewish Objections to Jesus, Volume 2*, 11.

[27] Ibid., 4; Cf. Tigay, 440 and his reference to *yihud* in Jewish theology.

that the Lord is *yachid*, meaning an absolute, solitary one—but rather that He is *echad*, a primary and composite one (cf. Proverbs 30:4).

"One" in the Greek Apostolic Scriptures

A proper understanding of "one" in the Greek Apostolic Scriptures and the nature of God must be understood in light of its Tanach background in the *Shema*. The Hebrew ADONAI *Eloheinu* ADONAI *echad* was rendered in the Greek Septuagint as *Kurios ho Theos hēmōn Kurios heis estin* (κύριος ὁ θεὸς ἡμῶν κύριος εἷς ἐστιν), "The Lord our God is one Lord" (LXE; cf. Mark 12:29). The Greek term corresponding to the Hebrew *echad* is *heis* (εἷς). The Greek *heis* has a wider array of connotations than does the Hebrew *echad*, as *echad* (אֶחָד) can be rendered as *heis* by the Septuagint, but not always. The Greek *heis* (εἷς) is much closer to the English term "one," with a range of meanings. "It usually means 'single,' 'once-for-all,' 'unique,' 'unanimous,' 'one of many,' or 'only one'" (*TDNT*).[28] This requires a reader to evaluate specific uses of *heis*, to determine what it actually means.

(Do be aware how the Greek language has three genders—masculine, feminine, and neuter—and is case driven, meaning that the forms of nouns, pronouns, and adjectives all change form and number given their function in a sentence or clause.[29] In the nominative case [indicating subject], the three main forms are the masculine *heis*, εἷς; feminine *mia*, μία; and neuter *hen*, ἕν. When we speak of the Greek term for "one" here, *heis* will be referred to, even though specific verses or clauses may have other forms used. Also not to be overlooked in Greek is the presence of the preposition *eis*, εἰς, often meaning "to" or "into," spelled exactly the same as the masculine εἷς for "one.")

In the examples referenced above from the Hebrew Tanach, where *echad* is employed to denote a oneness in plurality, the Greek Septuagint rendered *am echad* in Genesis 11:6 as *genos hen* (γένος ἕν) or "one race" (LXE), and *ish echad* in Numbers 14:15 as

---

[28] E. Stauffer, *"heis,"* in *TDNT*, 215.

[29] For a general review, consult David Alan Black, *It's Still Greek to Me* (Grand Rapids: Baker Books, 1998).

anthrōpon hena (ἄνθρωπον ἕνα) or "one man" (LXE). Both of these verses employ *heis* (εἷς) for one, indicating how *heis* can be used to represent composite groups of people as "one."

In the references provided by Kalland previously noted, we see how *echad* (אֶחָד) is rendered with *heis* (εἷς). *Ha'mishkan echad* (הַמִּשְׁכָּן אֶחָד) in Exodus 26:6 is rendered by the LXX as *hē skēnē mia* (ἡ σκηνὴ μία), and *v'hayah echad* (וְהָיָה אֶחָד) in Exodus 26:11 is rendered by the LXX as *kai estai hen* (καὶ ἔσται ἕν). Further, we see that *etz echad* (עֵץ אֶחָד) in Ezekiel 37:17, 19 is rendered by the LXX as *hrabdon mian* (ῥάβδον μίαν), and *goy echad* (גּוֹי אֶחָד) in Ezekiel 37:22 is rendered by the LXX as *ethnos hen* (ἔθνος ἓν).

Just like the Hebrew *echad*, the usage of the Greek *heis* (εἷς), in specific instances, will determine whether or not it represents composite groups of "one." In Romans 12:5, we definitely see *heis* used to denote a composite group of one, as Paul says, "so we, who are many, are **one body** in Messiah, and individually members **one of another**," *hen sōma esmen en Christō, to de kath' heis allēlōn melē* (ἓν σῶμά ἐσμεν ἐν Χριστῷ, τὸ δὲ καθ' εἷς ἀλλήλων μέλη). The Body of Messiah is made up of individual people, who are to serve one another in unity, *and* this unity is obviously a plurality of persons.

It is also to be noted that with Biblical Greek possessing a wider vocabulary than Biblical Hebrew, the Septuagint does not always translate *echad* (אֶחָד) as *heis* (εἷς). A notable instance in the LXX, where we have previously examined where *echad* is used, is Genesis 8:13, *b'echad l'chodesh*, "on the first of the month." This is rendered as *tou prōtou mēnos* (τοῦ πρώτου μηνός), "in the first month" (LXE), with the word *prōtos* (πρῶτος) or "first" employed.

In Psalm 68:6, where *yachid* (יָחִיד) is used to refer to "the solitary" (NJPS) or "the lonely," the LXX uses *monotropos* (μονότροπος), "the solitary" (LXE). If God in the *Shema* were to be considered an absolute one, rather than using the words *heis*, or even *prōtos* in the Greek, a term like *monos* (μόνος) could have surely been used instead.[30] However, what the Septuagint's

---

[30] The term *monos* is employed to describe exclusive service to the God of Israel in the Septuagint (1 Samuel 7:3) and Apostolic Scriptures (Matthew 4:10; Luke 4:8).

Jewish translators did, was render *ADONAI Eloheinu ADONAI echad* as *Kurios ho Theos hēmōn Kurios heis estin*, "The Lord our God is one Lord." In doing so, they helped to affirm that the God of Israel is the one and only God. A term with some ambiguity present to it, *heis* (εἷς), was used for "one."

Whenever the Greek term *heis* (εἷς) is used, context determines its proper meaning. However, we can to an extent carry the meaning of *echad* over into *heis*, where *heis* is employed in the Apostolic Scriptures. *Heis*, just like *echad*, can certainly be used to speak of a composite one and not an absolute one. There are places witnessed in the Apostolic Scriptures, where *heis* (εἷς) as a reference to the One God of Israel in the *Shema* of Deuteronomy 6:4, is specifically applied to Yeshua the Messiah. This is important for not only recognizing a plural Godhead of at *least* Father and Son, but also in establishing how Yeshua the Messiah is integrated directly into the Divine Identity, being every bit as much God as the Father.

1 Corinthians 8:5-6
The Messianic Shema: One God and One Lord

"For even if there are so-called gods whether in heaven or on earth, as indeed there are many gods and many lords, yet for us there is *but* one God, the Father, from whom are all things and we *exist* for Him; and one Lord, Yeshua the Messiah, by whom are all things, and we *exist* through Him."

Generally, all readers of 1 Corinthians are aware of the complicated circumstances that the Apostle Paul had to address, as his audience was significantly factionalized (cf. 1 Corinthians 1:11-13), and there were a significant number of issues plaguing them. Much of the Epistle of 1 Corinthians was composed as part of an ongoing correspondence between Paul and the Corinthian Believers, with 1 Corinthians actually being the second letter he had sent to them (1 Corinthians 5:9). Much of the dialogue, that occurred between Paul and the Corinthians in this letter, is seen with the Apostle arguing much of his position on the basis of logic—as it is quite possible that his non-extant letter argued from Tanach Scripture and was largely dismissed.[31] Among the important topics needing to be discussed, in 1 Corinthians, was the issue of meat taken from idol sacrifices. What was to happen in the event that any of the Corinthians ate meat that had been sacrificed to idols? Paul describes the situation in view:

"Now concerning things sacrificed to idols, we know that we all have knowledge. Knowledge makes arrogant, but love edifies. If anyone supposes that he knows anything, he has not yet known as he ought to know; but if anyone loves God, he is known by Him" (1 Corinthians 8:1-3).

Is it further stated by Paul how "concerning the eating of things sacrificed to idols, we know that there is no such thing as an idol in the world, and that there is no God but one" (1 Corinthians 8:4), *kai hoti oudeis Theos ei mē heis* (καὶ ὅτι οὐδεὶς θεὸς εἰ μὴ εἶς). Paul was not one to deny the real existence of dark supernatural forces, nor was he one to deny the insistence of the Apostolic decree which decisively forbade the new, non-Jewish Believers from eating meat sacrificed to idols (Acts 15:19-21). Yet, what if a Believer *ever* did eat meat sacrificed to idols? Ultimately, idols are just dead gold, silver, stone, and wood. The One God of Creation is superior to all, as He is the One who actually *created* the powers that pagans consider to be their gods.

In the event that a Corinthian Believer might eat meat sacrificed to idols, forgiveness from Him would surely be available. However, we can see that Paul did not at all endorse the Corinthian Believers going out and eating meat sacrificed to idols. He chides the Corinthians who think they can do this without any ensuing consequences, calling it "this liberty of yours" (1 Corinthians 8:9),[32] because by going out and associating

---

[31] For a summary of composition data, consult the entry for 1 Corinthians in the author's workbook *A Survey of the Apostolic Scriptures for the Practical Messianic.*

[32] The statement of, "But food will not commend us to God; we are neither the worse if we do not eat, nor the better if we do eat" (1 Corinthians 8:8), is likely one of the multiple Corinthian slogans that Paul had to confront in 1 Corinthians. The worst of them by far was *panta moi exestin* (πάντα μοι ἔξεστιν), "Everything is permissible for me" (1 Corinthians 6:12 & 10:23, NIV).

with those who eat meat sacrificed to idols, younger and weaker Believers may relapse into paganism (1 Corinthians 8:7-13).

Why the Apostle Paul can assert the supremacy of the One God of Israel is affirmed in an extremely important way, as is seen in 1 Corinthians 8:5-6:

"For even if there are so-called gods whether in heaven or on earth, as indeed there are many gods and many lords, yet for us there is *but* one God, the Father, from whom are all things and we *exist* for Him; and one Lord, Yeshua the Messiah, by whom are all things, and we *exist* through Him."

There is no doubting in Paul's mind that the idols the pagans of Corinth served were to classify as so-called "gods" and "lords." These were real demonic entities, composing the dominion of Satan—but were ultimately nothing in view of the Supreme Creator. However, for the righteous, Paul asserts that there is One God for them to serve, worship, and obey. In 1 Corinthians 8:6, though, the Apostle Paul is witnessed reworking the *Shema* of Deuteronomy 6:4, as not only does he testify that there is One God, the Father—but that there is also One Lord, Yeshua the Son. This is the Deity to whom all of the righteous are to pay heed. Notice the discernible linguistic connections between Deuteronomy 6:4 in the Septuagint, and how its language has been appropriated to apply to both the Father and Son:

Deuteronomy 6:4 (LXX): *Kurios ho Theos hēmōn Kurios* **heis** *estin* (κύριος ὁ θεὸς ἡμῶν κύριος εἷς ἐστιν)

1 Corinthians 8:6: *All' hēmin* **heis Theos ho Patēr** *ex ou ta panta kai hēmeis eis auton, kai* **heis Kurios Iēsous Christos** *di' ou ta panta kai hēmeis di' autou* (ἀλλ' ἡμῖν εἷς θεὸς ὁ πατὴρ ἐξ οὗ τὰ πάντα καὶ ἡμεῖς εἰς αὐτόν, καὶ εἷς κύριος Ἰησοῦς Χριστὸς δι' οὗ τὰ πάντα καὶ ἡμεῖς δι' αὐτοῦ)

In various theological circles, it has been witnessed that 1 Corinthians 8:6 has been known as a kind of "Christian *Shema*,"

For a more detailed analysis, consult the analyses for 1 Corinthians 6:12 and 1 Corinthians 10:23 in the author's book *The New Testament Validates Torah*. Also consult the author's article "The Message of 1 Corinthians."

in that the One God of Israel and the One Lord Yeshua the Messiah are identified side by side with one another. The relationship that the Father and the Son have, is presented by Paul in terms of the monotheistic declaration of the Deuteronomy 6:4 *Shema*. The Son is the Father's agent of Creation to be sure (John 1:3; Colossians 1:15-17), but He is identified in 1 Corinthians 8:6 as the One Lord, *heis Kurios* (εἷς κύριος). What makes this important, of course, is how the title *Kurios* was employed in the Greek Septuagint for rendering the Divine Name YHWH/YHVH (יהוה)—**a status applied directly to the Messiah!** The memorial name of the Eternal God, which was revealed to Moses at the burning bush (Exodus 3:15), is something that is possessed by the Messiah (cf. Philippians 2:10-11). In the view of Gordon D. Fee, we see how,

"In the same breath that he can assert that there is only one God, [Paul] equally asserts that the designation 'Lord,' which in the OT belongs to the one God, is the proper designation of the divine son. One should note especially that Paul feels no tension between the affirmation of monotheism and the clear distinction of the two persons of Father and Jesus Christ."[33]

The early Believers affirmed the Son's relationship to the Father in terms of the Son being the LORD or YHWH of the Deuteronomy 6:4 *Shema!* In recent Christological studies, this has been explained as the Son being integrated into the Divine Identity of the Godhead. Bauckham states that for 1 Corinthians 8:6, "Paul rewrites the Shema' to include both God and Jesus in the unique divine identity,"[34] which would obviously force a person to recognize how Yeshua the Messiah is to be considered the LORD God, and not just some kind of supernatural exalted being, yet ultimately not being God. Yeshua's integration into the Divine Identity, presented in terms of the *Shema*, would guard against any idea that the early Believers thought that there were multiple gods in the Heavenlies, but obviously that the One God

---

[33] Gordon D. Fee, *New International Commentary on the New Testament: The First Epistle to the Corinthians* (Grand Rapids: Eerdmans, 1987), 375.

[34] Richard Bauckham, *Jesus and the God of Israel* (Grand Rapids: Eerdmans, 2008), 213.

of Israel involved more than the Father. Bauckham further explains,

"In stating that there is one God and one Lord, Paul is unmistakably echoing the monotheistic statement of the Shema' ('YHWH our God, YHWH, is one'), whose Greek version in the Septuagint reads: *kurios ho theos hēmōn kurios heis estin.* He has, in fact, taken over all of the words of this statement, but rearranged them in such a way as to produce an affirmation of both one God, the Father, and one Lord, Jesus Christ...The only possible way to understand Paul as maintaining monotheism is to understand him to be including Jesus in the unique identity of the one God affirmed in the Shema'...Paul is not adding to the one God of the Shema' a 'Lord' the Shema' does not mention. He is identifying Jesus as the 'Lord' (YHWH) whom the Shema' affirms to be one. This, in Paul's quite unprecedented reformulation of the Shema', the unique identity of the one God *consists of* the one God, the Father, *and* the one Lord, his Messiah (who is implicitly regarded as the Son of Father)."[35]

The Father to be regarded as the One God, and the Son as the One Lord (*Kurios*/YHWH), would require not only Yeshua the Son to be considered Deity—but would also require the Godhead to be plural. The language proposed by a scholar like Bauckham, that the Son shares the same Divine Identity as His Father, is to be greatly appreciated. While Divine agency is involved in this, as the Son obeys the Father and submits to the Father—the Son is seen to be identified with titles that would have normally been exclusively reserved for the Father.

The Truth About the Trinity and Messianic Handling of the Shema

When one encounters the subject of the plurality of *Elohim* or God in much of today's Messianic movement, there is no shortage of statements or Messianic writing and literature that will denounce the historic Christian doctrine of the Trinity—that God is composed of Father, Son, and Holy Spirit—as somehow

[35] Ibid., pp 112-113.

being "pagan." For some reason or another, any possible parallel or detectable connection to another religion, as small as it might be—of God being composed of Father, Son, and Holy Spirit—means that the concept is to be flat rejected. This is a problem, because the historic doctrine of the Trinity is one of a *multitude* of potential beliefs that can be rejected via such a method, because of possible parallels or connections with paganism. There are scores of possible connections to be made between the early chapters of the Book of Genesis, and Ancient Near Eastern mythology—yet there is no widespread clamor in the current Messianic movement to say that the Noahdic Flood is really just the Epic of Gilgamesh repackaged into Israel's Scriptures.[36] Flippantly claiming that something is just outright "pagan," often without any substantial evidence, has been used far too frequently in today's Messianic movement to reject things that are legitimately communicated by the Bible.[37]

Of course, the fact that the doctrine of the Trinity is something that specifically developed in the Second-Fourth Centuries C.E., with much of the Christian Church having been cut off from its Hebraic Roots, leads a great number of Messianic people to treat it with some suspicion. Some are prone to reject any doctrine or belief that originated in Christendom, precisely because it is Christian. Others, however, know that this is inappropriate, because the Christian Church of the Second-Fourth Centuries C.E. used the same Holy Scriptures—both the Tanach and Apostolic Writings—that we use today. Millard J. Erickson properly advises all of us, "While those who give

---

[36] This is discussed further in the author's article, "Encountering Mythology: A Case Study From the Flood Narratives."

[37] It has to be noted that Outreach Israel Ministries and TNN Online, against the more common convention seen in much of the Messianic movement, have never argued that the holidays of Christmas and Easter are "pagan," per se. What we have instead argued is that these *holidays* are non-Biblical, because the *events* that they are intended to commemorate, the birth of the Messiah and His resurrection, are Biblical. We have preferred to state things along the lines of Christmas on 25 December and an Easter Sunday significantly divorced from the Passover, "not being God's original intention."

Consult the relevant sections of the *Messianic Winter Holiday Helper* and *Messianic Spring Holiday Helper* by TNN Press.

special authority to church councils have their authoritative answer [about the Trinity], that answer does not necessarily suffice for those Christians who do not consider the pronoucements of the church councils infallible."[38] **Our attention needs to be placed squarely upon the Biblical text,** to see if the concept of a God composed of Father, Son, and Holy Spirit is something that can be legitimately derived from Scripture.

Much of the confusion, that can arise from Bible readers wondering where a doctrine of some Trinity appears in Scripture, is that they typically look for a specific formula of *Father, Son, and Holy Spirit* to be found. It is widely recognized that today, the so-called Johannine Comma of **1 John 5:7-8** in the Textus Receptus,[39] is unoriginal to what was originally written, which was, "For there are three that testify: the Spirit and the water and the blood; and the three are in agreement."[40] However, the immersion formula of **Matthew 28:19**, "Go therefore and make disciples of all the nations, baptizing them in the name of the Father and the Son and the Holy Spirit," is something which is not unoriginal to the ancient copies of Matthew's Gospel,[41] and it has been argued on theological grounds by some that immersing in Father, Son, and Holy Spirit is a theme that

---

[38] Millard J. Erickson, *Making Sense of the Trinity: Three Crucial Questions* (Grand Rapids: Baker Books, 2000), 15.

[39] "For there are three that bear record in heaven, the Father, the Word, and the Holy Ghost: and these three are one" (1 John 5:7-8, KJV).

[40] Bruce M. Metzger, *A Textual Commentary of the Greek New Testament* (London and New York: United Bible Societies, 1975), pp 715-717.

[41] R.T. France, *New International Commentary on the New Testament: The Gospel of Matthew* (Grand Rapids: Eerdmans, 2007), 1117 states, "There is...no evidence that this is not an original part of the Gospel of Matthew." For a Messianic evaluation of this, consult the article "In the Name of the Father and the Son and the Holy Spirit: Matt 28:19 – A Later Addition to Matthew's Gospel?" by Tim Hegg, available for access at <www.torahresource.com>.

It cannot go unnoticed that the Shem Tov Hebrew Gospel of Matthew, which various Messianics think is superior to the canonical Greek Matthew, does lack any reference to Father, Son, and Holy Spirit in Matthew 18:19. The Shem Tov Matthew, though, was put together from a Jewish anti-missionary work entitled *Even Bohan* (אבן בוחן), and dates from the Fourteenth Century C.E. An evaluation of the Shem Tov Matthew is provided in the author's article "Is the Hebrew Matthew an Authentic Document?" (forthcoming).

naturally arises from what has been communicated by Matthew's Gospel.[42]

It would be too simplistic for any Bible reader to think, though—as those who oppose any doctrine of God being composed of Father, Son, and Holy Spirit commonly do—that these are the only two places in the Apostolic Scriptures where Father, Son, and Holy Spirit are seen functioning together. While the formula *Father, Son, and Holy Spirit* is not always used as such, there are a selection of passages in the Apostolic Scriptures where these manifestations of the Godhead are seen functioning together, and co-existing side by side:

> "Now there are varieties of gifts, but the same **Spirit**. And there are varieties of ministries, and the same **Lord**. There are varieties of effects, but the same **God** who works all things in all *persons*" (1 Corinthians 12:3-4).

> "The grace of the **Lord Yeshua the Messiah**, and the love of **God**, and the fellowship of the **Holy Spirit**, be with you all" (2 Corinthians 13:14).

> "*There is* one body and one **Spirit**, just as also you were called in one hope of your calling; one **Lord**, one faith, one baptism, one **God and Father** of all who is over all and through all and in all" (Ephesians 4:4-6).

> "But we should always give thanks to **God** for you, brethren beloved by the **Lord**, because **God** has chosen you from the beginning for salvation through sanctification by the **Spirit** and faith in the truth. It was for this He called you through

---

[42] In the view of John Nolland, *New International Greek Testament Commentary: The Gospel of Matthew* (Grand Rapids: Eerdmans, 2005), 1269,

"The choice of language is well rooted in earlier Matthean language. So it seems natural to think of Matthew as taking up important strands of the story he has been telling. In 1:1 Matthew summarized in a triad of names the genealogy to follow, by means of which he defined Jesus in relation to the history of God's prior dealings with his people. Now at the end Matthew sums up his own narrative and identifies in briefest compass the significance of his chief protagonist by speaking of Jesus as the Son in relation to the Father and as closely linked with the Holy Spirit. Matthew's story has been about the action of the Father through the Son and by means of the Holy Spirit."

our gospel, that you may gain the glory of our **Lord Yeshua the Messiah**" (2 Thessalonians 2:13-14).

"Peter, an apostle of **Yeshua the Messiah**, To those who reside as aliens, scattered throughout Pontus, Galatia, Cappadocia, Asia, and Bithynia, who are chosen according to the foreknowledge of **God the Father**, by the sanctifying work of the **Spirit**, to obey **Yeshua the Messiah** and be sprinkled with His blood: May grace and peace be yours in the fullest measure" (1 Peter 1:1-2).

"John to the seven churches that are in Asia: Grace to you and peace, from Him who is and who was and who is to come, and from the seven **Spirits** who are before His throne, and from **Yeshua the Messiah**, the faithful witness, the firstborn of the dead, and the ruler of the kings of the earth. To Him who loves us and released us from our sins by His blood—and He has made us *to be* a kingdom, priests to His **God and Father**—to Him *be* the glory and the dominion forever and ever. Amen" (Revelation 1:4-6).

If you were to remove Matthew 28:19, the customary immersion formula, from your deliberations, you will still have to reckon with the above passages, which give us significant clues about the composition of God. Is it at all reasonable to conclude that a plural *Elohim* or God is composed of the co-existent manifestations of Father, Son, and Holy Spirit? There is ample evidence from the Biblical text that those who affirm the doctrine of the Trinity are *not* on unsafe ground. They have had to make decisions that affirm the Son as Divine, and the Holy Spirit as something separate from the Father, as both being integrated into the Godhead along with the Father. At the same time, when one sees references to "the seven Spirits who are before His throne" (Revelation 1:4), or to "a spiritual rock which followed them; and the rock was Messiah" (1 Corinthians 10:4)—it might be said that the historic Christian doctrine of the Trinity can be *incomplete* in a few areas. A Godhead composed of Father, Son, and Holy Spirit being *incomplete*, however, is a *far cry* from the Trinity being pagan. Working with the Biblical evidence, rather than to conclude that *Elohim* or God is *only*

Father, Son, and Holy Spirit—it might instead be that *Elohim* or God is *widely* demonstrated to us as Father, Son, and Holy Spirit. As mortal human beings, none of us wants to ever find ourselves placing inappropriate limits on our Eternal God, and conclude that there are no other manifestations of Him beyond Father, Son, and Holy Spirit.

A great deal of Messianic Judaism to the present time has never had a problem with viewing the plurality of *Elohim* (אֱלֹהִים) as being *at least* composed of Father, Son, and Holy Spirit.[43] Messianic Judaism has demonstrated some aversion to using the term "Trinity," as employed by much of Christianity, and instead preferred—and we should think rightfully so—to use valid alternative terminology like **tri-unity**, or perhaps in some cases, **revealed tri-unity**. Such terms would align with the Biblical evidence that God is composed of the co-existent persons or manifestations of Father, Son, and Holy Spirit—but it does not discount the possibility, or even probability, that there is more to God which has been largely disclosed to mortals. A rather recent perspective is offered by Barney Kasdan in his commentary *Matthew Presents Yeshua, King Messiah* (2011). Remarking on Matthew 28:19, "Therefore, go and make people from all nations into *talmidim*, immersing them into the reality of the Father, the Son and the *Ruach HaKodesh*" (CJB), he summarizes,

> "...While Messianic Jews affirm the concept of the tri-unity of the one God, we may not necessarily agree with [some of] the Greek words and explanation [historically offered]...Undoubtedly some of the Hebrew background would have made a great contribution to this doctrinal discussion. Even though it is good and proper to ask some deeper questions about the nature of God, we should emphasize that Yeshua himself called the *Sh'ma* the greatest commandment (cf. Mark 12:28-34). One thing is for sure: Whatever the New Testament teaches about the pluralistic

---

[43] Michael Schiffman, "Messianic Jews and the Tri-Unity of God," in John Fischer, ed., *The Enduring Paradox: Exploratory Essays in Messianic Judaism* (Baltimore: Lederer, 2000), pp 61-69; Brown, *Ansering Jewish Objections to Jesus, Volume 2*, pp 52-59.

aspect of the one God, it must be consistent with the full revelation of the *Tanakh* (cf. Matthew 5:17).

"Some conclusions from a Messianic Jewish perspective lead us to view God as One and yet as a mysterious plurality within that unity. This is reflected in the words of the Great Commission of Yeshua, as the disciples are to go 'in the Name' (reality) of *the Father, the Son, and the Ruach HaKodesh*. It must be pointed out that even with the mention of the three realities of God, Yeshua uses the singular word 'name' in describing all three. This is consistent with the mystery of the one God revealed in a plurality of manifestations."[44]

It is absolutely true that there are others in Messianic Judaism, as well as the One Law/One Torah and Two-House sub-movements, who would repudiate the idea that the *Elohim* or God of Israel can reveal Himself to humanity in the co-existent persons or manifestations of Father, Son, and Holy Spirit. Where this has Biblical evidence, tends to be lacking. Where this has emotional evidence, as though everything that the historic Christian Church has believed is to *always* be rejected, is something quite plentiful. Yet for all of us, **our loyalty should be to whether or not a God composed of** (at least) **Father, Son, and Holy Spirit can be reasonably deduced from the Biblical text.**

If I had to answer "yes" or "no" to the question, "Do you believe in the Trinity?", I would answer "yes." If I could explain myself following this question, I would add that "God might be more than the Trinity, though." This is why *Elohim* (אֱלֹהִים) or God might be better considered to be a **revealed tri-unity**, or to

---

[44] Barney Kasdan, *Matthew Presents Yeshua, King Messiah: A Messianic Commentary* (Clarksville, MD: Lederer Books, 2011), pp 396-397.

It cannot be overlooked in the case of both Schiffman, in Fischer, 69 and Kasdan, 396, that they have referred to the Zohar and its assertion of there being "three heads" of God. While this could be used as a reference to claim that the idea of the One God of Israel made up of three persons or manifestations is not incompatible with Jewish theology, the Zohar originates from the Middle Ages and is thus not reflective of the Jewish theology of the broad First Century—much less the fact that the Zohar is a main work of the Kabbalah and Jewish mysticism. This is why we should think that Bauckham's approach in *Jesus and the God of Israel*, of Yeshua being integrated into the Divine Identity of the LORD or YHWH, better corresponds to views present within the broad First Century period, and to the Biblical text itself.

adapt traditional Christian terminology, a **principal trinity**. To deny that God is surely composed of Father, Son, and Holy Spirit—is to go against what has been communicated to us in Holy Scripture, and how it is to mold the worldview of Believers. In all likelihood, *there is more* to our Eternal God that goes beyond the co-existent manifestations or persons of Father, Son, and Holy Spirit that would, at the very least, confuse us as limited mortals. Many evangelical Christians I know would be open to this, because God, after all, is far bigger and more wonderful than any of us can humanly imagine. At present, much of who God is and how He has acted in human history, has to be left as a mystery, something yet to be revealed to us until the Eternal State.

That there is One God, as the *Shema* of Deuteronomy 6:4 commands us to believe, cannot be denied. For Believers in the Messiah of Israel, we are to recognize Him as the One Lord, as His early followers did (1 Corinthians 8:6), with Yeshua integrated into the Divine Identity. And beyond this, that there is more to the composition of *Elohim* or God, can surely be recognized, even if much of it remains a mystery to us at present.

Answering the
"Frequently Avoided Questions"
About the Messiahship
of Yeshua

answering the claims of the anti-missionary movement

The Messianic community of faith presently finds itself at a very serious crossroads, not just a crossroads in determining its long term purpose and where it is going to be in the next few decades, but most seriously in its theology and how we are to approach the Bible. The enemy desperately wants us to get off course and away from the mission of seeing the restoration of the Kingdom to Israel accomplished (Acts 1:6). He wants us to not be a movement of positive change and transformation, where people are empowered by the Lord to accomplish His tasks in the world—but rather be one of mischief, confusion, and apostasy. The enemy wants us to seriously "mess up" and gain a bad reputation so that people will (rightly) stay away.

One of the most significant ways that this has happened over the past several years has been seen when various Messianic individuals deny the Divinity of Yeshua the Messiah. There have been both Messianic teachers and laypersons who have decided that Yeshua the Messiah was nothing more than a human being empowered by God, but certainly not God in the flesh. They have stripped away the reality of His Incarnation, and made Him little more than a mortal like one of "us."

It is not all that surprising, but among a significant number of those who deny Yeshua's Divinity **are those who later deny His Messiahship.** Not content with their entirely human Yeshua, these people then question whether or not Yeshua is even the Messiah and whether they truly need Him. Outsiders to the Messianic community who witness this trend, often believe that the Messianic movement is *not* something that God has raised up to restore the lost Hebraic Roots of the faith, or even just see a generation of Jewish people brought to Yeshua—but rather is a move of the Adversary to lead people *away* from the salvation available in Yeshua and the truth of the gospel. Is this truly the case? Are we nothing more than a revolving door, leading people into our midst for a short season, and then into the open arms of a Messiah-less Synagogue?

What are some of the "frequently avoided questions" about Yeshua's Messiahship that we must answer to prevent any further apostasy? How might the issue of Yeshua's Messiahship shake us out of our complacency in other areas of theology?

Who have we invited into the camp?

There have always been obstinate arguments present in the Jewish world against the Messiahship of Yeshua. The testimony of the Gospels is clear that many Jews in the First Century rejected Yeshua as the Messiah. The testimony of history is likewise clear that many Jews throughout the centuries rejected Him as well. Some of the reasons as to why Yeshua was rejected are complicated. On the one hand, many who encountered Yeshua and His Disciples wanted nothing to do with them for ideological reasons or because they found their message of repentance offensive. On the other hand, many Jews throughout history have rejected Yeshua because of the unfortunate politicization of much of the Medieval Christian Church, and grossly misguided laws and persecution imposed by anti-Semitic leaders.[1] Certainly, the Church has played a large role in Jewish

---

[1] Note that we need not make any broad or overly-simplistic conclusions regarding the complicated history of relations between the Jewish people and the Christian Church. While it is very true that the Church has been directly responsible for atrocities against the Jews (which have largely been renounced by modern

rejection of Yeshua, but it is not solely to blame. The defiant will of any person—Jewish or otherwise—in rejecting the gospel is just as responsible.[2]

Fast forwarding to today, through the rise of Messianic Judaism in the Twentieth Century, and now with many Christians eagerly examining their Hebraic Roots, a sector of Jewish teachers commonly known as "anti-missionaries" have arisen. These anti-missionaries specifically target Messianic Jews and Christians interested in their Hebraic Roots *for (re)conversion to Judaism* and to denounce Yeshua as Messiah.

Anti-missionary organizations and teachers originate mainly from the Orthodox branch of Judaism. What makes this significant, in combating their arguments, is in knowing that Orthodox Jewish theology is largely sectarian, its hermeneutics can, at times, often be overly simplistic, and it is usually isolationist. Orthodox Jewish examination of the Tanach is frequently devoid of external discussion regarding history, comparative linguistics with cognate languages of Biblical Hebrew, and factors relating to Ancient Near Eastern society.

It cannot be ignored that anti-missionary teachers and organizations tend to sit at the far Right end of the theological spectrum. They often hold to extreme views regarding the composition of the Tanach that cannot be substantiated in the larger field of Biblical Studies. Has the Torah been preserved *perfectly* stroke-by-stroke since Mount Sinai *without any* textual deviations of any kind? Are issues such as time, place, location,

---

Christian leaders), it is also very true that there were many Christians who stood against these atrocities as well. **Having a fair minded view of the issues is absolutely imperative.** We cannot discount the fact that these poor relations have equally been a Jewish problem as they have been a Christian problem, as the Jewish community was often not open to reasoned dialogue and discussion any more than the Christian community was often not open to moderate and cordial relations with their Jewish neighbors.

Consult the author's article, "The Top Ten Urban Myths of Today's Messianic Movement" for a further discussion. Also consult the balanced and realistic remarks of Michael L. Brown, *Answering Jewish Objections to Jesus, Volume 1: General and Historical Objections* (Grand Rapids: Baker Books, 2000), pp 124-145.

[2] I would also emphasize here that even though many Jews have rejected Yeshua, *ultimately*, only God Himself knows the heart condition and eternal destiny of **any person**—Jewish or non-Jewish.

and contemporary history to be considered *irrelevant* when determining not only the meaning of a Biblical text, but also a text's reliability? These are some major issues where the Orthodox Jewish scholarship employed by anti-missionaries comes up severely short.

Just to see a common example of the style of interpretation we will respond to, consider a rather "mundane" issue presented by Exodus 1:8: "Now a new king arose over Egypt, who did not know Joseph." Why is this the case? Surely, with all of the exploits of Joseph seen in Genesis chs. 39-50 as a political leader in Egypt, this new king would have known of Joseph. Messianics commonly struggle over this passage, often not knowing how to interpret it. Often turning to Orthodox Jewish resources like the *ArtScroll Chumash*, they are confronted with explanations such as the following:

"Either it was literally a new king, or an existing monarch with 'new' policies, who found it convenient to 'ignore' Joseph's monumental contributions to the country (*Sotah* 11), probably on the grounds that whatever the Jew Joseph had done for Egypt was ancient history and no longer mattered. This 'what have you done for me lately' kind of anti-Semitism is another familiar phenomenon of Jewish history."[3]

Certainly, while there are many good things that one can glean from Orthodox Jewish Bible scholarship, this explanation for the Pharaoh not knowing Joseph is not one of them (including Joseph being anachronistically called a "Jew," as the term *Yehudi*, יְהוּדִי was not readily used until after the Babylonian exile). Are we to honestly think that the new king of Egypt did not "know" (Heb. *yada*, יָדַע) Joseph in some kind of *intimate way*, meaning that he just casually did not acknowledge Joseph's accomplishments? Or, are we to consider the first possibility: that a new king arose over Egypt from a new dynasty who did not *factually* know of Joseph? It is clear which position the *ArtScroll Chumash* takes: the subjective interpretation. The exegesis represented here takes the "easy path."

---

[3] Nosson Scherman, ed., et. al., *The ArtScroll Chumash, Stone Edition*, 5th ed. (Brooklyn: Mesorah Publications, 2000), 293.

The objective interpretation, though, forces us to take the "hard path." It forces us to consider not only the text of Exodus 1:8, but also the possible Egyptian historical backdrop. We have to consider events that may have occurred between the time of Joseph and the sons of Jacob entering into Egypt, and the installation of this new king over Egypt. Non-Orthodox Jewish scholarship (and much of Christian scholarship) does not ignore these critical factors and is engaged in a much larger conversation. As Jewish commentator Nahum M. Sarna summarizes,

"The most reasonable explanation for the change in fortune lies in the policies adopted by the pharaohs of the Nineteenth Dynasty (ca. 1306-1200 B.C.E.), and especially by Ramses II (ca. 1290-1224 B.C.E.), who shifted Egypt's administrative and strategic center of gravity to the eastern Delta of the Nile."[4]

Sarna gives a further clue on his commentary for Exodus 1:9-10 as to why the Egyptians may have been fearful of the Ancient Hebrews:

"The eastern Delta of the Nile was vulnerable to penetration from Asia. In the middle of the eighteenth century B.C.E. it had been infiltrated by the Hyksos, an Egyptian term meaning 'rulers of foreign lands.' The Hyksos were a conglomeration of ethnic tribes among whom Semites predominated. They gradually took over Lower Egypt and ruled it until their expulsion in the second half of the sixteenth century B.C.E."[5]

A new Pharaoh of Egypt from a new dynasty could have easily not known of Joseph because the Israelites settled in Goshen, in the Nile Delta region of Lower Egypt or Northern Egypt, and as Pharaoh he would have been from Upper Egypt or Southern Egypt, moving back into previously conquered territories. Wanting to rebuild an empire that had been diminished, the Israelites having multiplied would make a convenient workforce. Politically it would have been easy to

---

[4] Nahum M. Sarna, *JPS Torah Commentary: Exodus* (Philadelphia: Jewish Publication Society, 1991), 4.

[5] Ibid., 5.

enslave them, because as Semites they would remind many Egyptians of the Hyksos invasion.

I give this illustration because ignoring the critical factors of history, setting, and to a lesser degree linguistics, is seen throughout much Orthodox Jewish examination of the Tanach. God has given us all minds and reasoning skills so that we might be joined to a large and much more modern theological conversation. The anti-missionaries, in contrast, often set themselves off to the side, isolating themselves in a theological vacuum. We should not be shocked to see that the factors of history, setting, and linguistics are often not employed in their criticisms of the Apostolic Scriptures or New Testament. **If they are not of the habit of employing these things in how they examine the Tanach, they will certainly not be employed when examining the Apostolic Scriptures and life of Yeshua.** (Ironically enough, in many cases they ignore some of their own literature which reflects various interpretations and opinions regarding key Messianic texts.)[6]

It should also not be surprising to us when we see that the greatest influence of the anti-missionary movement takes place among (former) Messianics who strongly lean toward an Orthodox style, or even some kind of more fundamental form, of Torah *halachah*.[7] Messianics who separate themselves in a spiritual and social vacuum, often not interacting with other Messianics or with other people in general, are those who are most susceptible to the anti-missionary arguments. Some of them are open because they feel that they will be fully accepted by the Synagogue, and others are open because they have bitterness and

---

[6] Michael L. Brown's *Answering Jewish Objections to Jesus* series provides many of these references in relation to Biblical passages and historical Jewish interpretations, many of which go beyond the intended scope of this article.

[7] Please note that these comments should *not* be interpreted as meaning that I am opposed to mainline Jewish tradition (such as the Karaites, who often practice the same kind of disengaged exegesis as Orthodox Judaism) or a conservative approach to Torah *halachah*. What it is to say is that a *halachah* leading to isolationism and non-interaction with society at large is wrong, and these are generally things not seen in the more Centrist branches of Judaism.

Consult the relevant sections of the *Messianic Torah Helper* by TNN Press (forthcoming).

hatred toward anyone who is not a part of their clique (primarily Christians).

While the Messianic movement will probably always have the nagging annoyance of the anti-missionaries to deal with, it will only remain at "crisis proportions" until the theology of the broad Messianic community can progress more significantly toward the Center and away from the extreme Right. Answering the claims against Yeshua's Messiahship is complicated because of the current tensions that exist in Messianic theology, the realm of our hermeneutics (how we examine and interpret Scripture), our approach to the larger Jewish (and to a lesser extent, Christian) world, and whether or not we are engaged in the much larger theological "conversation."

Likewise, in examining the Messiahship of Yeshua, things are complicated because too many Messianic teachers make the mistake of believing that *only* the Hebrew source text of the Tanach is sufficient for Biblical examination. Too many fall into the serious error (and indeed urban myth) of believing that the Masoretic Text (MT) used in today's Orthodox Judaism, and which is also the primary text used for most English Bibles' translation of the Tanach or Old Testament, has been copied without deviation or any kind of variance since antiquity.[8] *We should not be so naïve.* Not enough Messianics are aware of the fact that the final form of this text dates from the Seventh-Tenth Centuries C.E., a minimum of seven hundred years *after* the ministry of Yeshua—and certainly a long way from the Exodus and Mount Sinai.[9] While we will indeed be considering the Hebrew of the MT in our primary examination of Yeshua's Messiahship, our analysis *will by no means* disclude the textual witnesses of the Greek Septuagint (LXX), Latin Vulgate, or Dead

---

[8] We recommend that if you use a Hebrew text for the Tanach, that you have a critical text like the *Biblia Hebraica Stuttgartensia* (Stuttgart: Deutche Bibelgesellschaft, 1977). While this text reads practically identical to the Rabbinical text of today, it does offer in its footnotes alternate readings that appear in the Greek Septuagint, Latin Vulgate, Aramaic Targums, Dead Sea Scrolls, and other ancient translations and manuscript sources.

[9] Cf. E.J. Revell, "Masoretic Text," in David Noel Freedman, ed. et. al., *Anchor Bible Dictionary*, 6 vols. (New York: Doubleday, 1992), 4:597-599.

Sea Scrolls (DSS), and linguistic studies beyond that of Biblical Hebrew.

The narrow minded anti-missionary reliance upon only the MT is strong evidence that they are not part of a larger theological, and indeed, textual conversation. One common anti-missionary tactic is to claim that the Apostolic Scriptures misquote from the Hebrew Tanach. To a certain extent this is not incorrect; the Apostolic Scriptures do not quote from a Seventh-Tenth Century C.E. Hebrew text that did not exist in the First Century C.E. The Apostolic Scriptures largely employ the Greek LXX, and may even rely upon some of its *interpretive value judgments* to make theological points. Acts 15:17 is an excellent example of this, where James the Just quotes from the Prophet Amos at the Jerusalem Council:

"SO THAT THE REST OF MANKIND MAY SEEK THE LORD, AND ALL THE GENTILES WHO ARE CALLED BY MY NAME."

The Hebrew MT in Amos reads slightly different:

"So that they shall possess the rest of Edom and all the nations once attached to My name—declares the LORD who will bring this to pass" (Amos 9:12, NJPS).

The difference between what James says and the Hebrew text in Amos, is that James follows the Septuagint rendering which reads with *hoi kataloipoi tōn anthrōpōn* (οἱ κατάλοιποι τῶν ἀνθρώπων) for the Hebrew *sh'eirit Edom* (שְׁאֵרִית אֱדוֹם). The LXX translators understood *Edom* (אֱדוֹם) to be connected to *adam* (אָדָם), also the Hebrew word for "**mankind, people**" (*HALOT*),[10] and rendered it in Greek as "the remnant of men" (Apostle's Bible) or "those remaining of humans" (NETS), referring to God's faithful remnant that would come forth out of humanity's masses. James makes the connection between the salvation of Israel and those of the nations coming to faith in Israel's Messiah.

Far too many of today's Messianic people do not have a high regard for the Greek Septuagint, or for that matter Greek language studies in general. They find themselves as easy prey for those who claim that the Apostolic writers misquote from the Tanach, when in actuality the Apostolic writers are often just

---

[10] *HALOT*, 1:14.

quoting from the Septuagint.[11] We do have to make the value judgment whether or not the LXX—**the oldest complete witness to the Scriptures of Israel**—plays a role in our Messianic theology and exegesis. Many decide a definite "no," and they are the same ones who are often led to reject Yeshua's Messiahship. But we should know better, because Israel is supposed to be God's conduit by which the entire world can be blessed (Genesis 22:18; Deuteronomy 4:5-8), and by necessity one must communicate to the world in languages other than Hebrew to fulfill this Divine mandate.[12]

Unfortunately, when we look at some of the things resulting from an Orthodox Jewish style of *halachah* in our midst today, and what the anti-missionaries have done to the Messianic world, we have some serious things to consider and (re)evaluate. Some Messianics have to remove themselves from their isolationism and begin to consider things not only that have been left out of the conversation regarding interpretation of the Apostolic Scriptures, but *also* have been ignored regarding the Tanach itself. When we do this, we find that the Messiahship of Yeshua, while being one of the most serious issues in our faith— is uniquely connected to other issues that we commonly avoid. **I do not believe that God will let us avoid these things any longer.**

Can we be entirely "objective"?

When one encounters the arguments of anti-missionaries, such teachers do not hide the fact that they have a bias. It is a firm teaching of Orthodox Judaism that one cannot be a Jew and believe in Yeshua. Centuries of Christian teaching only reinforced this concept from the other side, as one could not be a

---

[11] Not realizing this fact has already caused a sector of Messianics to doubt and disregard the canonicity of the Epistle to the Hebrews, whose author makes over thirty-two direct quotations from the LXX. For a further review, the author's article "The Message of Hebrews," and his commentary *Hebrews for the Practical Messianic*.

[12] Consult the author's article "Can We Trust the Greek Scriptures?" Also consult R. Timothy McLay, *The Use of the Septuagint in New Testament Research* (Grand Rapids: Eerdmans, 2003).

Christian and a Jew at the same time. Only until the advent of Messianic Judaism in the Twentieth Century would one be able to even have a concentrated "anti-missionary movement," ready to go out and stop Jews en masse from hearing about the Messiah. What has made Messianic Judaism so radical is that it affirms that a Jewish person can be a Believer in Yeshua the Messiah, and still retain his or her Jewishness. But while Christian positions on the Jewishness of Jewish Believers have greatly moderated, the same cannot really be said for Jewish positions on the Jewishness of Jewish Believers.

Things are more complex today with large numbers of non-Jews entering into the Messianic movement. For some reason or another, many non-Jewish Believers are experiencing great spiritual fulfillment in Messianic congregations and fellowships. They are learning things about their faith that were not discussed in their previous church settings. They are discussing commonly overlooked Scriptures. They are learning about the Jewishness of Jesus and about the richness of His teachings. To the anti-missionary, these people make prime targets for conversion.

Certainly, the anti-missionary, who wants to see the numbers of Orthodox Judaism increase, has a definite agenda and bias. He will prey on the ignorance of a Believer in Yeshua to get him or her to renounce faith in Him. This is compounded when a Messianic teacher may be responsible for presenting an unbalanced amount of attention to Orthodox Jewish views of the Tanach—notably at the expense of the more moderate branches of Judaism—and constantly repudiates Christian Bible teachers and the Christian Church. People can then begin to idolize "the Rabbis," and find themselves led down a path to apostasy. It is no different than what Paul tells the Galatians about the Influencers: "They eagerly seek you, not commendably, but they wish to shut you out so that you will seek them" (Galatians 4:17). These "Rabbis" are not people who are open to dialogue with Believers in Yeshua, but they certainly want Believers in Yeshua to seek out their opinions so they can be swayed away from Him.

I do not want to be seen as anti-Jewish by any means in these remarks, but much of today's broad Messianic movement often lacks realism and pragmatism when it comes to "the

Rabbis." The anti-missionaries capitalize on this time and time again, and Messianic teachers who are unbalanced to our *shared* spiritual and theological heritage coming from both Judaism *and* Christianity only add to the problem. The anti-missionaries are not objective and their aims at getting people to deny our Lord and Savior are never hidden.

Those of us who affirm Yeshua's Messiahship should certainly strive to be as objective as possible, unlike the anti-missionaries. We should strive to be part of a larger theological conversation, *not* ignoring the factors that anti-missionaries commonly ignore. Yet, in that objectivity we should plainly recognize that **one's spirituality does play a distinct role in believing whether or not Yeshua is the Messiah.** A person in a Messianic congregation will often be unprepared to encounter anti-missionary tactics and arguments. Someone may ask a random question at a Bible study from a website or e-mail they have read, or worse yet an actual anti-missionary may surreptitiously visit your congregation. What does a person do when backed up against a wall, having to respond to arguments he or she has never heard before? Are you to capitulate and give in?

I can only answer for myself. While I have certainly had enough theological training to know that things are never as simplistic as anti-missionaries often make them, the spiritual forces at work via the anti-missionaries are quite severe. It is not as though the anti-missionaries are just misguided people; they have a mission from Satan himself.[13] It is not as though these people are interested in reasoned and constructive dialogue trying to find some common ground (as many other Jewish people may be); they want your soul. A Believer in Yeshua—when backed up against the wall by anti-missionary arguments—**must fall back on his or her spiritual experience with God via His Son Yeshua.**

---

[13] I do not hesitate to tell the reader that I believe that the Jewish anti-missionary movement is likely "the synagogue of Satan" seen in Revelation 3:9. Consult the chapter of *When Will the Messiah Return?*, "The Philadelphian Assembly."

The end-time saints described in Revelation overcome Satan "because of the blood of the Lamb **and because of the word of their testimony**, and they did not love their life even when faced with death" (Revelation 12:11). Anyone, be they anti-missionaries or atheists wanting Believers to deny Yeshua, must ultimately be overcome via our personal testimonies of salvation. When anti-missionary ideas or the people themselves infiltrate your ranks, you may not have time to respond to their arguments. No matter how much study or preparation you have had, you may not be able to anticipate all of their arguments. **You must stand confident in your relationship with God via His Son.**

On August 8, 1995 I had a profound supernatural encounter with the God of Israel. I had just returned from a Christian youth camp where the Ten Commandments were emphasized throughout the week as God's standard of holiness. Returning home, I was unsure of my spiritual condition or whether or not I was even "saved." I spent several hours in my bedroom confessing my violation of the Ten Commandments before God. *These were* **some** *several hours.* Not only did I feel forgiven of my sins, but demons that had been allowed to influence me manifested themselves, and I was shown the reality of the eternal, *never-ending* judgment that awaited me separated from God's presence.[14] **I always fall back on my experience when attacks are issued against my faith.** I do not claim total objectivity, because having a supernatural encounter with the Creator God is never something totally objective. *I do not hide my bias.*[15]

If we have a deep seated assurance of our salvation, then responding to the arguments of those who would steal our redemption is only a matter of study and time. And, given the

---

[14] Consult the author's article "The Assurance of Our Salvation" for a further discussion of the importance of God's commandments in the salvation process. Also consult the relevant sections of the author's article "Why Hell Must Be Eternal."

[15] Of course, we should all be reminded of the fact that the most biased issue that human beings have to consider is whether or not there is a Supreme Being who created the universe. Answering the question, "Is there a God?" is *most definitely affected* by one's experience, **just as much** as the question "Is Yeshua/Jesus the Messiah?"

largely disengaged perspective of the anti-missionaries, we find that this is often quite easy when we are equipped with the proper tools and data.

Answering these "Frequently Avoided Questions"

Time and space do not permit us to address all of the claims that are made against the Messiahship of Yeshua. Indeed, new reasons are being proposed all of the time as the Messianic community grows and the anti-missionary movement becomes more virulent. **Many of the issues have to be considered in yet-to-be-written Messianic commentaries on books of the Bible.** Still, there are some significant claims that are commonly made by anti-missionaries about the life of Yeshua, prophecies that He supposedly did not fulfill, and supposed misapplications of Tanach texts by the Apostolic writers. These claims easily upset and disturb Messianic Believers, who often do not have a readily available answer to them. The claims that we will answer in our analysis largely relate to these areas. We have limited them to the common ten claims that usually circulate—so-called "frequently avoided questions"—that are often asked of our ministry by those who encounter anti-missionary works.

You will find that there are relatively easy answers to most of the claims that are made today by anti-missionaries against the Messiahship, and indeed the ministry of Yeshua of Nazareth. However, many of these claims are also innately connected to other Biblical issues. So, in offering responses to claims that are made against our Lord and Redeemer, each of us—whether a teacher or layperson—is going to be challenged in other areas of our theology. Surely, if the Messianic movement is indeed something that God is going to use for some great things in the future, He is going to make sure that we are a mature people *who can handle **any** issue.*

False Claim #1

Numbers 23:19 clearly states that God is not a man, yet Christianity considers Jesus to be God, when at most he was just a human teacher.

A bridge between denying Yeshua's Divinity and later His Messiahship is often built by anti-missionaries quoting Numbers 23:19 to a person who fails to consider the setting and context in which its words are given. Seeds of doubting the Messiahship of Yeshua are planted, as it may seem that Christian expositors have misunderstood the Gospels and have inappropriately given Jesus of Nazareth a status that He was never intended to have. But this is not what Numbers 23:19 says.

The setting of this verse is the Torah portion *Balak* (Numbers 22:2-25:19), when King Balak of the Moabites commissions the prophet-for-hire Balaam to curse the people of Israel. The narrative of Numbers 23, specifically, includes a dialogue between the Lord and Balaam, including a word that Balaam is to give Balak (23:7-10), and Balak arguing with Balaam about him not cursing Israel (23:11-15). After carrying on a dialogue with God (23:16), Balaam issues the following words to Balak:

"Arise, O Balak, and hear; give ear to me, O son of Zippor! **God is not a man, that He should lie, nor a son of man, that He should repent; has He said, and will He not do it? Or has He spoken, and will He not make it good?** Behold, I have received *a command* to bless; when He has blessed, then I cannot revoke it. He has not observed misfortune in Jacob; nor has He seen trouble in Israel; the LORD his God is with him, and the shout of a king is among them. God brings them out of Egypt, He is for them like the horns of the wild ox. For there is no omen against Jacob, nor is there any divination against Israel; at the proper time it shall be said to Jacob and to Israel, what God has done! Behold, a people rises like a lioness, and as a lion it lifts itself; it will not lie down until it devours the prey, and drinks the blood of the slain" (Numbers 23:18-24).

In Numbers 23:19, the false prophet Balaam, speaking the words of God, says "God is not a man, that he should lie, nor a son of man, that he should change his mind. Does he speak and then not act? Does he promise and not fulfill?" (NIV). Anti-missionaries make good on someone's ignorance of the context of the passage which has *nothing to do* about the makeup or composition of God, but has everything to do with the character of God. Numbers 23:19 is an excellent example of where an inclusive language translation for *lo ish El* (לֹא אִישׁ אֵל) and *u'ben adam* (וּבֶן־אָדָם) can actually make the text much clearer. Numbers 23:19 speaks of the fact that "God is not a **human being**, that he should lie, or a **mortal**, that he should change his mind" (NRSV).[16]

Even though "Son of Man" is a title used by Yeshua to refer to Himself frequently throughout the Gospels, Numbers 23:19 employs *ben adam* or "son of man" in a way comparable to "mortal" (NJPS), referring to the fact that when God makes a decision He follows through on it not repenting or changing His mind. This is clear given the fact that Balaam testifies to Balak of God's blessing Israel, something that He is not going to change given His previous actions of leading Israel out of Egypt and preserving them in the wilderness. God not being a man or a mortal is substantiated where His perfect character is contrasted to the limitations of humans. (Also to be considered can be God's restraint in judgment seen in Hosea 11:9, where He says "For I am God and not man [for I am God and no mortal, NRSV], the Holy One in your midst, and I will not come in wrath.")

Contrary to how "son of man" is used in Numbers 23:19, Yeshua no doubt employed the title "Son of Man"[17] for Himself via its Danielic usage (Daniel 7:9-14), where Daniel is shown the throne room of God. The Prophet says, "I kept looking in the night visions, and behold, with the clouds of heaven One like a Son of Man [Ara. *bar enash,* בַּר אֱנָשׁ] was coming, and He came up to the Ancient of Days and was presented before Him." The context here is not Earthly, but rather is clearly Heavenly, representing one at the right hand of God. I.H. Marshall validly remarks, "the Danielic background suggests a figure closely associated with the Ancient of Days....Jesus took over this sense

---

[16] The NJPS has the similar, "God is not man to be capricious, or **mortal** to change His mind."

[17] Grk. *ho huios tou anthrōpou* (ὁ υἱὸς τοῦ ἀνθρώπου).

of the phrase, and thus identified his role with that of the figure in Daniel 7."[18] Yeshua notably uses the title "Son of Man" to describe His return to the Earth (Matthew 24:30; Mark 13:26; Luke 21:27) and thus His dominion over "all the peoples, nations and *men of every* language" (Daniel 7:14).

While "son of man" can be a reference to human beings as appears in Numbers 23:19, Yeshua's usage of this title for Himself is substantially different. We need not be confused by anti-missionaries who not only misquote Numbers 23:19 out of context, when the passage deals with the character of God, but by those who fail to see a broader view of the title "Son of Man" in relation to one intimately involved with the Ancient of Days.

False Claim #2
Psalm 22:17(16) uses "lion" and not "pierced" in the Hebrew. Christian Bibles have purposefully mistranslated the verse to prove the Messiahship of Jesus.

Psalm 22 is a significant text as it relates to the crucifixion and subsequent death of Yeshua. So significant is it, that Derek Tidball observes in his book *The Message of the Cross*, "Certainly the Gospel writers could not read it without thinking of the cross of Christ. Not only did its opening words form the wrenching cry of dereliction that came from the lips of Jesus as he died, but also the manner of his death, in detail after detail, seems to be prophesied here."[19]

Yeshua quotes this psalm's opening words, "My God, my God, why have You forsaken me?" (Psalm 22:1) while suffering on the cross (Matthew 27:46; Mark 15:34). While it may seem that Yeshua has been "forsaken" by His Father, Psalm 22 is actually attributed to David of his entreating God for His vindication of righteous action (vs. 23-31). The text has some definite parallels with specific actions of the life of Yeshua, including a reference to garments being divided up after lots are cast (vs. 18-19; cf.

[18] I.H. Marshall, "Son of Man," in *Dictionary of Jesus and the Gospels*, 781; cf. Tim Hegg, *The Messiah: Introduction to Christology* (Tacoma, WA: TorahResource, 2006), pp 53-68.
[19] Derek Tidball, *The Message of the Cross* (Downers Grove, IL: InterVarsity, 2001), 85.

Matthew 27:35; Mark 15:24; Luke 23:34; John 19:24). Likewise, the words "let Him [God] deliver him" (v. 8) were hurled at Yeshua as He was dying on the cross (Matthew 27:39-43).

Psalm 22:16 is significant as it says in the NASU, "For dogs have surrounded me; a band of evildoers has encompassed me; **they pierced my hands and my feet.**" In referring to the suffering of our Lord, we can certainly see the significance of this verse relating to His crucifixion. Indeed, the imagery of being "pierced" features throughout the Messianic expectation and hope of the Apostolic Scriptures (Isaiah 53:5; Zechariah 12:10; John 19:34).

Certainly, Psalm 22 has some parallels to the life of King David, but as Walter C. Kaiser validly asks, "what events in David's life might provide the background for the abject status before all people mentioned in verse 6? When were his hands and feet pierced (assuming that is the proper reading of v. 16) and his garments divided among his detractors (v. 18)?"[20] This is certainly not a text that anti-missionaries want connected to the life of Yeshua and His death on the tree.

Anti-missionaries commonly use Psalm 22:16 to say that Christian Bibles deliberately manipulate this verse to prove the Messiahship of Yeshua. Indeed, as this verse reads in the ATS version, "For dogs have surrounded me; a pack of evildoers has enclosed me, **like** [the prey of] **a lion are my hands and my feet.**" The MT Hebrew clearly reads *hiqqiphuni ka'ari yadai v'raglai* (הִקִּיפוּנִי כָּאֲרִי יָדֵי וְרַגְלָי).

It is notable that Psalm 22:16(17) has issues that are easily seen when one compares the MT to the witnesses of the LXX and Vulgate. Tim Hegg points out that *hiqqiphuni ka'ari yadai v'rag'lai* "is pointed by the Masoretes to read 'like a lion my hands and my feet.' כָּאֲרִי is taken to be the particle -כְּ, 'like' or 'as' plus the noun, אֲרִי 'lion.' The Lxx, however, reads the word as כָּאֲרוּ or כָּרוּ (or something similar), a third person plural perfect verb of a speculated root כאר as related to כור or כרה…The Aramaic verb כער, 'to make ugly,' 'to disfigure,' or Hebrew כרה, 'to dig' and by

[20] Walter C. Kaiser, *The Messiah in the Old Testament* (Grand Rapids: Zondervan, 1995), 112.

analogy, 'to pierce,' corresponds to the Lxx ὀρύσσω, 'to dig, pierce.'"[21]

Indeed, the LXX of Psalm 22:16 reads with *ōruxan cheiras mou kai podas* (ὤρυξαν χεῖράς μου καὶ πόδας), "they pierced my hands and my feet" (LXE), followed by the Vulgate's *foderunt manus meas et pedes meos*, "They have dug my hands and feet" (Douay Rheims). Kaiser notes that these are the oldest available readings,[22] and new manuscript discoveries confirm the authenticity of the underlying Hebrew originally being the verb *karu* (כָּרוּ) or "they dug," by extension meaning "they pierced." Hegg summarizes,

"Scraps from a scroll containing some of the Psalms were discovered at Nachal Hever, and one scrap contained the line from Psalm 22:16 with the word in question well in view. Though the writing on the scrap was faint, under magnification it was easy to see and decipher. The word clearly ended in a *vav* [ו] not a *yod* [י], and was therefore a 3rd person plural verb: 'they dug' or 'they pierced.' Here was evidence that the Lxx translators had not 'fooled' with the text, but had faithfully translated the Hebrew original that was before them. Since this scrap is dated (in accordance with the style of letters used) to 50-68 CE, it is almost 1000 years earlier than the Masoretic text, and shows that in at least one of the earliest Hebrew traditions of Psalm 22, the word is not 'like a lion' but 'they dug' or 'pierced.'"[23]

Only if one is constrained to the straightjacket of the Hebrew MT of Psalm 22:16(17) exclusively in Biblical exegesis, as the anti-missionaries are, can a person be convinced that "like lions *they maul* my hands and feet" (NJPS) is the correct reading. The ancient witnesses of the LXX, Vulgate, and now textual evidence from Nachal Hever attests to the reading "they pierced My hands and feet" (NASU). Psalm 22 is a very important section of Scripture that reflects the suffering of Yeshua, and His ultimate

---

[21] Tim Hegg, *Messiah in the Tanach* (Tacoma, WA: TorahResource, 2003), 139.

[22] Kaiser, *The Messiah in the Old Testament*, 115, fn#10.

[23] Tim Hegg (n.d.). *Psalm 22:16—"like a lion" or "they pierced"? Torah Resource.* Retrieved 07 October, 2007, from <http://www.torahresource.com>.

Cf. Michael L. Brown, *Answering Jewish Objections to Jesus, Volume 3: Messianic Prophecy Objections* (Grand Rapids: Baker Books, 2003), pp 123-127.

vindication. We need not follow a simplistic method of examination as do those who deny Him, but one where we investigate all textual avenues.[24]

False Claim #3
Matthew 2:23 is wrong. There is no single prophecy that states that the Messiah will be called a Nazarene.

Matthew 2:23 records that Yeshua the Messiah "came and lived in a city called Nazareth. *This was* to fulfill what was spoken through the prophets: 'He shall be called a Nazarene.'" The challenge for some interpreters is the fact that no specific text is being quoted. This is not unusual to see in the Apostolic Scriptures by any means. Yeshua Himself says in Matthew 26:54, "How then will the Scriptures be fulfilled, *which say* that it must happen this way?" Here, the Messiah is speaking of the general sense or meaning of the Tanach, not necessarily a specific verse. In James 4:5 we see a similar usage: "Or do you think that the Scripture speaks to no purpose: 'He jealously desires the Spirit which He has made to dwell in us'?" Here, James appeals to the general sense of Scripture from the Tanach, rather than a specific verse or prophecy.

In Matthew 2:23, the author references the "prophets," indicating that he is appealing to a theological concept evidenced in several places in the Tanach, *not* a single prophecy as anti-missionaries try to mislead people to believe. What is actually being communicated by the statement, "He will be called a Nazorean" (NRSV), has been a cause of great discussion and some debate among Bible interpreters and commentators.

What is likely being communicated by Matthew is some kind of word play on the terms *nazir* (נָזִיר), primarily meaning "(s.one) dedicated, consecrated" (*CHALOT*),[25] by extension "a nazirite," and the word "Nazarene" (Grk. *Nazōraios*, Ναζωραῖος), meaning someone from the city of Nazareth. An adequate

---

[24] For a further examination of Psalm 22, consult Kaiser, *The Messiah in the Old Testament*, pp 111-118.

[25] William L. Holladay, ed., *A Concise Hebrew and Aramaic Lexicon of the Old Testament* (Leiden, the Netherlands: E.J. Brill, 1988), 232.

description of a nazirite is given to us in Judges 13:7, where Samson's mother is told how her son is to live:

"But he said to me, 'Behold, you shall conceive and give birth to a son, and now you shall not drink wine or strong drink nor eat any unclean thing, for the boy shall be a Nazirite to God from the womb to the day of his death.'"

The Hebrew *ki-nezir Elohim yihyeh* (כִּי־נְזִיר אֱלֹהִים יִהְיֶה) was rendered two different ways in the Greek Septuagint, both of which would have been extant in the First Century. The LXX(a) version has *naziraion Theou* (ναζιραῖον θεοῦ) or "nazirite of God," whereas the LXX(b) version has *hagion Theou* (ἅγιον θεοῦ), "holy to God" (LXE). This attests to the fact that being a "holy one" of God and a "nazirite" of God were considered to be interconnected sometime before the First Century. One did not necessarily have to take a "nazirite vow" to be considered a holy person, which there is no record of Yeshua ever doing. In Mark 1:23-24 we see Yeshua being *Nazarēne* (Ναζαρηνέ, adjective) or "of Nazareth" connected to His holiness:

"Just then there was a man in their synagogue with an unclean spirit; and he cried out, saying, 'What business do we have with each other, Yeshua of Nazareth? Have You come to destroy us? I know who You are—the Holy One of God!'"

Matthew, seeing this concept referred to in Mark's Gospel, whose audience was largely Roman and would have overlooked any connection between "Nazareth" and "Holy One," is likely expounding upon this for his Jewish audience, possibly using additional source material.[26] His Jewish audience would have been familiar with the terms *nazir*, or the Septuagint renderings of *naziraion Theou* or *hagion Theou*. Matthew's emphasis, more than anything else, is to connect the concept of Yeshua being a Nazarene to His holiness. Notably, one does not necessarily have to take a "nazirite vow" to be considered holy, though as Hegg notes, "Yeshua's words at the last Pesach [Passover], that He would not drink of the fruit of the vine until He came into His

---

[26] Consult the author's entries for the Gospels of Mark and Matthew in *A Survey of the Apostolic Scriptures for the Practical Messianic*, for a further description of these texts' composition.

kingdom, are reminiscent of the Nazirite prohibition against eating or drinking anything from the vine. The same may be said of Yeshua's refusal to accept the wine while on the cross."[27]

A second, and more commonly proposed view espoused by many Messianics, is that Matthew is making some kind of word play on *netzer* (נֵצֶר), meaning "**sprout, shoot** (of plant)" (*CHALOT*),[28] or by extension "branch." This would have probably been a commonly known Hebrew word in the First Century among both Jews in Israel and the Diaspora, and *does not* require that Matthew would have had to compose his Gospel in Hebrew. It is commonly connected to prophecies such as Isaiah 11:1:

"Then a shoot will spring from the stem of Jesse, and a branch [*netzer*] from his roots will bear fruit."

This prophecy has been viewed in a Messianic context by the Jewish Sages,[29] and is appealed to various times by the Apostles (Romans 15:12; 1 Peter 4:14; Revelation 5:5). One of the challenges with holding *exclusively* to this view, though, is the fact that other Messianic prophecies applying to Yeshua employ the Hebrew term *tzemach* (צֶמַח) for "branch":

"'Behold, *the* days are coming,' declares the LORD, 'When I will raise up for David a righteous Branch [*tzemach*]; and He will reign as king and act wisely and do justice and righteousness in the land" (Jeremiah 23:5).

"In those days and at that time I will cause a righteous Branch [*tzemach*] of David to spring forth; and He shall execute justice and righteousness on the earth" (Jeremiah 33:15).

---

[27] Hegg, *Matthew: Chapters 1-7*, 70.

[28] *CHALOT*, 244.

[29] One does not have to go far to see this reflected in contemporary Orthodox Jewish opinion. The reference notes in the *ArtScroll Tanach* attest to Isaiah 11:1 being a Messianic prophecy:

"The Ten Tribes, which were exiled by the Assyrians, will also be redeemed by the future Messiah, who will descend from the son of Jesse i.e., David (*Rashi*)" (Nosson Scherman and Meir Zlotowitz, eds., *ArtScroll Tanach* [Brooklyn: Mesorah Publications, 1996], 972).

"Now listen, Joshua the high priest, you and your friends who are sitting in front of you—indeed they are men who are a symbol, for behold, I am going to bring in My servant the Branch [*tzemach*]" (Zechariah 3:8).

"Then say to him, 'Thus says the LORD of hosts, "Behold, a man whose name is Branch [*tzemach*], for He will branch out from where He is; and He will build the temple of the LORD" (Zechariah 6:12).

We can certainly consider the words *netzer* and *tzemach* to be synonyms, as the latter likewise means "**growth, what sprouts**," "**shoot, bud**" (*CHALOT*).[30] This would account for Matthew's reference to "the prophets," as opposed to a singular prophet (cf. Isaiah 11:1). Matthew, more than anything else, relies on his audience's knowledge of knowing that the terms *nazir*, *naziraion*, and "holy one" are all connected with Yeshua being a "Nazarene." The major point that Matthew emphasizes is that Yeshua has been separated out as the Father's appointed servant and is the ideal of holiness, and being holy unto God or sanctified is certainly a theme epitomized in the Prophets. Hegg validly states, "Yeshua, in all of His life lived out the quintessential meaning of the Nazirite vow, for He was the Holy One of God in every way."[31] One need not go very far to understand this connection and how it makes Yeshua a "Nazarene."

Anti-missionaries are able to lead people astray by getting them to think that *one prophecy=one fulfillment* is what is communicated by the Gospel authors. In some cases, a specific prophetic reference may certainly be made by the Gospel authors. But in other cases, however, a *general understanding* of prophetic texts may also have to be considered. The Gospel authors consider Yeshua of Nazareth to be the epitome of the Hebrew Tanach, and that He embodies in His person the fullness of the qualities of holiness communicated by its Prophets.[32] Note

---

[30] *CHALOT*, 307.

[31] Hegg, *Matthew: Chapters 1-7*, 71.

[32] Matthew's statement "*This was* to fulfill what was spoken through the prophets" (2:23), likely referring to several verses seen in the Prophets, applying

that if Matthew is primarily building his case for Yeshua being a "Nazarene" from Judges 13:7, that the Book of Judges is considered a part of the *Nevi'im* or "the Prophets" in the traditional Jewish order of the Tanach (whereas Christian tradition places it among the Historical Books). Has Matthew misapplied Scripture, or are Jewish anti-missionaries trying to oversimplify things?

False Claim #4
Matthew 2:15 has deliberately misapplied Hosea 11:1, as it calls the people of Israel out of Egypt, not Jesus out of Egypt.

In the narrative describing the birth, infancy, and young childhood of Yeshua, Matthew's Gospel records how Joseph and Mary had to flee to Egypt as King Herod was seeking to kill Him:

"Now when they [the magi] had gone, behold, an angel of the Lord appeared to Joseph in a dream and said, 'Get up! Take the Child and His mother and flee to Egypt, and remain there until I tell you; for Herod is going to search for the Child to destroy Him.' So Joseph got up and took the Child and His mother while it was still night, and left for Egypt" (Matthew 2:13-14).

Joseph, Mary, and the Child Yeshua were able to flee to Egypt because Egypt in the First Century had a huge Jewish

---

them to Yeshua, is immensely more responsible than some of the so-called prophecies often referred to in Orthodox Jewish scholarship today.

In Genesis 14:14 we are told that Abraham pursued Lot's captors "as far as Dan." If we accept exclusive Mosaic authorship of the Torah, as all Orthodox Jews do (and far too many Messianics do), how on Earth would Moses have known to write "Dan" as a place name in Genesis when the possession of Canaan had yet to occur? The most commonly held view is that since Moses was a prophet he prophesied the name of this place into being. Yet, this is a very unlikely possibility. "Dan" is a place name; Genesis 14:14 is not a prophecy that is intended to speak of a future event or a prophecy by which people return to God.

Far be it from Genesis 14:14 being the result of either the so-called J or E source of the Pentateuch, conservatives who accept Mosaic composition have widely recognized this verse as including an aMosaic reference, likely appended at a later date, possibly even after the Babylonian exile via the authorization of Ezra the Priest.

For a further discussion, consult the author's entry for the Book of Genesis in *A Survey of the Tanach for the Practical Messianic*.

community where they could find refuge. In the next verse, Matthew records that King Herod dies, making it safe for Joseph, Mary, and the Child Yeshua to return to Judea:

"He remained there until the death of Herod. *This was* to fulfill what had been spoken by the Lord through the prophet: 'OUT OF EGYPT I CALLED MY SON'" (Matthew 2:15).

The specific text referenced by Matthew is Hosea 11:1: "When Israel *was* a youth I loved him, and out of Egypt I called My son." The entire Book of Hosea is largely a lament by the Prophet of the sins and rebellion of the Northern Kingdom.[33] We see references in Hosea to God's work in delivering Israel, and how Ephraim has been responsible for disregarding His deliverance. Hosea 11:2 summarizes that after God called Israel out of Egypt, "The more they called them, the more they went from them; they kept sacrificing to the Baals and burning incense to idols." Having delivered Israel via the Exodus, all the people can do is fall into sin.

The application of Hosea 11:1 to the Child Yeshua leaving Egypt asks the interpreter certain questions about the usage of prophetic typology. It has to be noted that Hosea's word "out of Egypt I called My son" is not isolated, as in Numbers 24:8 it is asserted "God brings him [Israel] out of Egypt." Clearly in both Numbers and Hosea, the historical, collective people of Israel— "God's son" as they are called—are being referred to. Hosea feels perfectly free to quote from the Torah, in a word delivered regarding a blessing of Israel, and may be viewed as applying it as a curse as Hosea 11:5 further says, "They will not return to the land of Egypt; but Assyria—he will be their king because they refused to return *to Me*." God delivers Israel, Israel refuses Him, and God must then punish His people, which in Hosea's case was specifically concerned with the Northern Kingdom.

In what sense does Matthew feel free to apply Hosea 11:1 to Yeshua? Is he justified in doing so? It absolutely must be noted that the ideas of First Century Messianism—whether applied to Yeshua of Nazareth or not—were profoundly affected by the

---

[33] Consult the author's entry for the Book of Hosea in *A Survey of the Tanach for the Practical Messianic*, as well as his article "The Message of Hosea."

broad themes of Ancient Israel's Exodus from Egypt. The coming Messiah was viewed as a Second Moses who would offer a greater deliverance that Moses did not provide. Can the Gospel writers take a particular theme in the history of Israel and then apply it to Yeshua of Nazareth? Rabbinical literature is affluent with examples of where past historical events are used to interpret more current events. C.A. Evans explains,

"Emphasis on the unity of Scripture and history is the distinctive of typological interpretation. What God has done in the past (as presented in Scripture), he continues to do in the present (or will do in the future). Recent events or future events that are interpreted as salvific are frequently compared to major OT events of salvation...Typological interpretation makes it possible for later communities of faith to discern the continuing activity of God in history. It is likely that these ideas lay behind the typologies that Jesus developed....Typological interpretation is not limited to the NT; it is also found in rabbinical writings...The messianic age is often compared with the Exodus, a comparison frequently developed by typological interpretation."[34]

In considering Hosea 11:1 to be a reference to Yeshua, who would return to Judea from Egypt, is Matthew doing something strange or irregular? The Rabbinical technique known as *gezera shava* would often link one or two vocabulary words in a text to make an important theological point or application. Matthew does this to not only connect "Egypt" to the return of Yeshua to Judea, but also "Son" — representing Israel — to Him. God commands Moses to declare to Pharaoh in Exodus 4:22 that "Israel is My son, My firstborn." Herod, a kind of "Pharaoh," has just died, and Yeshua is the Son who embodies the hopes and aspirations of Israel. Yeshua, as "Son" here represents the quintessential Israelite. By quoting Hosea 11:1, Matthew is trying to communicate critical ideas regarding the Exodus and necessarily *greater* deliverance that Yeshua will provide.

Matthew is only doing something strange or irregular if God's plan of salvation history is not repeated to some degree in

---

[34] C.A. Evans, "Typology," in *Dictionary of Jesus and the Gospels*, 863.

the persons or vehicles used to accomplish His purposes—whether through Yeshua or through other people. In the case of Yeshua, if the model of the Exodus is *to some degree* to be repeated in His life, then the typological application of Hosea 11:1 by Matthew to Yeshua returning from Egypt is certainly **not invalid**. It is a message from Matthew to those reading His Gospel, that the Son Yeshua, embodying the national hope of Israel, is One who must be heeded.[35] And, this hope is not only for those Jews in Judea, but concerns those of the exiled Northern Kingdom referred to in the Book of Hosea, and indeed the *entire world* of humanity at large. Yeshua has come to redeem all people from the curse!

False Claim #5
Jesus is not the "greater prophet" spoken of by Moses.

The message of Deuteronomy is one where Moses must repeat God's Instruction to Israel before He dies, as it recapitulates the story of the Exodus, the wilderness journey, and it issues some final words not seen in the previous four books of the Torah.[36] In Deuteronomy 18, in particular, Moses commands Israel not to fall into idolatrous ways (18:9-14), and then issues a word that a prophet like him will be raised up among the people:

"The LORD your God will raise up for you a prophet like me from among you, from your countrymen, you shall listen to him. This is according to all that you asked of the LORD your God in Horeb on the day of the assembly, saying, 'Let me not hear again the voice of the LORD my God, let me not see this great fire anymore, or I will die.' The LORD said to me, 'They have spoken well. I will raise up a prophet from among their countrymen like you, and I will put My words in his mouth, and he shall speak to them all that I command him. It shall come about that whoever will not listen to My words which he shall speak in My name, I Myself will require *it* of him'" (Deuteronomy 18:15-19).

The original word delivered by Moses to Israel assures the people that God will raise up a prophet to whom they must

---

[35] Cf. Hegg, *Matthew: Chapters 1-7*, pp 62-65.
[36] Consult the author's article "The Message of Deuteronomy."

heed. Moses serves as the prototype of this prophet. The people do not desire to have the Almighty God tell them *directly* what they must do as they cannot bear the thunder and smoke of Mount Sinai (cf. Exodus 20:18-19; Deuteronomy 5:23-27), and so He must send an intermediary. The uniqueness of Moses as a prophet for Ancient Israel is seen in the closing words of Deuteronomy:

"Since that time no prophet has risen in Israel like Moses, whom the LORD knew face to face, for all the signs and wonders which the LORD sent him to perform in the land of Egypt against Pharaoh, all his servants, and all his land, and for all the mighty power and for all the great terror which Moses performed in the sight of all Israel" (Deuteronomy 34:10-12).[37]

Numbers 12:6-8 speaks of the significance of Moses as a prophet:

"He said, 'Hear now My words: If there is a prophet among you, I, the LORD, shall make Myself known to him in a vision. I shall speak with him in a dream. Not so, with My servant Moses, He is faithful in all My household; with him I speak mouth to mouth, even openly, and not in dark sayings, and he beholds the form of the LORD. Why then were you not afraid to speak against My servant, against Moses?'"

Kaiser indicates, "all the other prophets missed something that Moses had because of his unique relationship with God. In this regard, then, this promise to Moses served to unite him with the coming one, the Messiah."[38]

But was Deuteronomy 18:15-19 actually a word viewed with some kind of Messianic overtones in the First Century? Note that people do ask John the Immerser, "Are you the Prophet?" (John 1:21); and after the feeding of the five thousand by Yeshua, people declare, "This is truly the Prophet who is to come into the

---

[37] The significance of this word is enhanced if it was inserted centuries after the original composition of Deuteronomy, during the time of Ezra the Priest when the final form of the Pentateuch was issued (cf. Kaiser, *The Messiah in the Old Testament*, 58 fn#22; b.*Sanhedrin* 21b). This would be a reflection on the fact that by the Sixth-Fifth Centuries B.C.E., the prophet of which Moses spoke still had not arrived.

[38] Kaiser, *The Messiah in the Old Testament*, 59.

world" (John 6:14). The testimony of the Gospel of John, at least, is that a Great Prophet was expected. The Apostle Peter's message at *Shavuot*/Pentecost directly appropriates the words of Deuteronomy 18:15-19 and applies them to Yeshua:

"Therefore repent and return, so that your sins may be wiped away, in order that times of refreshing may come from the presence of the Lord; and that He may send Yeshua, the Messiah appointed for you, whom heaven must receive until *the* period of restoration of all things about which God spoke by the mouth of His holy prophets from ancient time. Moses said, 'THE LORD GOD WILL RAISE UP FOR YOU A PROPHET LIKE ME FROM YOUR BRETHREN; TO HIM YOU SHALL GIVE HEED to everything He says to you. And it will be that every soul that does not heed that prophet shall be utterly destroyed from among the people'" (Acts 2:19-23).

Is the text of Deuteronomy 18:15-19 a direct, or even indirect, Messianic reference? 1 Maccabees 14:41 indicates that a little less than two centuries before Yeshua, "the Jews and their priests decided that Simon should be their leader and high priest for ever, until a trustworthy prophet should arise" (RSV). This shows us that there was some expectation of a future prophet arising in Israel. Likewise, in the Qumran document 4Q175 (or 4QTestimonia) from the Dead Sea Scrolls, the Qumran community connected selections such as Deuteronomy 5:28-29; 18:18-19; Numbers 24:15-17; and Deuteronomy 33:8-11 and interpreted them in a futuristic Messianic fashion.[39] Does Peter draw a misguided conclusion, applying Deuteronomy 18:15-19 to Yeshua, that has no precedent? It does not appear so, as Peter's conclusion that Yeshua is the Great Prophet is based within the opinions of his time.

In the original context of Deuteronomy 18:15-19, it may be that Moses' principal emphasis was that there is an office of prophet that will be filled when the people need someone to deliver a direct word from God to them. This prophet will call the people back to God and to obedience to Him. Certainly, many prophets in the history of Israel did this to some degree.

---

[39] Cf. Michael Wise, Martin Abegg, Jr., and Edward Cook, trans., *The Dead Sea Scrolls: A New Translation* (San Francisco: HarperCollins, 1996), pp 229-231.

Deuteronomy 18:15-19 need not have originally applied to the coming Messiah, as Hegg concludes it is "a general promise of the continuing prophetic office rather than a specific prophecy of the Messiah."[40] Yet, Yeshua Himself is considered by Peter to be the Great Prophet *par excellance* who entirely fulfills the purpose of the one spoken of by Moses who would fully reveal God's plan to Israel. Kaiser validly remarks, "each prophet became a type of the final prophet who was to appear,"[41] that Prophet being Yeshua of Nazareth.

The major anti-missionary discussion regarding Deuteronomy 18:15-19 often does not relate to whether or not this text had some Messianic significance in the First Century, which the Apostles can apply to Yeshua. On the contrary, it often relates to the surrounding verses, Deuteronomy 18:9-14 and 20-22. Anti-missionaries assert that Yeshua the Messiah led many Jews of the First Century astray by magic arts and witchcraft, and spoke presumptuously incurring the curse of a false prophet. The first accusation is clearly a value judgment made on the basis of not accepting His miracles as truly Divine works of God, as prophets in the Tanach are often seen performing miracles via God's power.[42] The second, that Yeshua made false predictions, is often made with support found in His words from the Olivet Discourse on the Last Days:

"Truly I say to you, this generation will not pass away until all these things take place" (Matthew 24:34; cf. Mark 13:30; Luke 21:32).

Anti-missionaries will often say that because the end-time events of Matthew 24, Mark 13, and Luke 21 did not occur in the First Century, that Yeshua of Nazareth was a false prophet. Interestingly enough, there are three major interpretations of Yeshua's words that exist among interpreters today that need to be considered:

---

[40] Hegg, *Messiah in the Tanach*, 74.

[41] Kaiser, *The Messiah in the Old Testament*, 61.

[42] What set Yeshua apart from the Prophets of the Tanach is that He was able to forgive sins (Mark 2:7), something that only God Himself could do, and many Jews of His time considered to be blasphemy. Not surprisingly, anti-missionaries consider Yeshua and His claim to be God (John 10:33) to be blasphemy.

1. The Lord says "this generation will not pass away," and is referring to the generation that lived during the time that He declared these words. Preterists who believe that the "end-times" actually took place during the First Century, and consider the antichrist of Revelation to be Nero Caesar, are the most common advocates of this view.

2. The Lord says "this generation will not pass away," and is speaking of a future group of people, which will be those who will witness all of the events prior to His return.

3. When the Lord refers to what the Greek records as *hē genea autē* (ἡ γενεὰ αὕτη), which in most Bibles is rendered as "this generation," He is not referring to a "generation" of people. As should be noted, *genea* has a variety of possible renderings, including "*race, stock, family*" and "*a race, generation*" (*LS*).[43]

Yeshua's words need not be interpreted regarding a specific "generation" that He either spoke to in the past, or is speaking to in the future, but rather an ethnic group of people that will have survived long enough into the future to be present to experience the end-times. Of the three options considered, the most probable could very well be that Yeshua actually referred to "this *race* will not pass away,"[44] a reference to the preservation of the Jewish people. Yeshua has not made a false prediction; anti-missionaries have just oversimplified one of His statements. (Of course, the interconnectivity of the Messiahship of Yeshua with other issues is fully realized because if "this *race* will not pass away" is indeed the valid viewpoint, it can significantly affect

---

[43] *LS*, 161.

[44] The *Ryrie Study Bible* actually confirms these conclusions, remarking, "No one living when Jesus spoke these words lived to see 'all these things' come to pass. However, the Greek word can mean 'race' or 'family,' which makes good sense here; i.e., the Jewish race will be preserved, in spite of terrible persecution, until the Lord comes" (ed. Charles C. Ryrie [Chicago: Moody Press, 1978], 1490).

some current opinions of eschatology seen in today's Messianic movement.)

Is Yeshua the epitome of not just all the Prophets of the Tanach, but of Moses himself? Was a prophet greater than Moses anticipated by the Jews of the First Century? Is Yeshua that Prophet? This can only be found in one understanding the true mission and purpose of Moses, the Prophets of the Tanach, and the ministry and service of Yeshua as seen in the Gospels. Today's Messianic community has a great responsibility in that we understand who our Lord actually is as typified by Moses and the Prophets, and that we truly understand who He is from His own teachings and actions. Unfortunately, in a Messianic movement too often dominated by "Torah study," these critical studies are largely yet to be performed to the degree they should have. Because they have yet to be performed, too many have become cannon fodder and are easily led astray by anti-missionaries.[45]

False Claim #6
The genealogies of Jesus in Matthew 1 and Luke 3 do not align with the genealogies of the Tanach.

Anti-missionaries are able to, unfortunately, have a great amount of success in disturbing Believers in claiming that the genealogies of Yeshua in Matthew 1 and Luke 3 do not somehow "properly correspond" with genealogies seen in the Tanach. What is most significant to consider when we see the distinct genealogies of Yeshua, as recorded in Matthew 1 and Luke 3, is that we cannot subject ancient genealogies to our Twentieth or Twenty-First Century Western expectations of exactness. While we would today expect a precise correlation between fathers, sons, grandsons, great-grandsons, etc.—genealogies seen throughout Scripture are often given to make an important point with the people who are listed, **and may not be as exact as the modern person would want them to be.**

---

[45] Likewise, there is severe deficiency in today's Messianic movement in understanding the epistles of the Apostolic Scriptures and how they instruct us on how to form productive and spiritually maturing communities of faith. Consult the author's article "Congregations Among Us" for a further discussion of this issue.

Modern genealogies are used today for the expressed purpose of communicating one's descent and family history. Many people living in North America, for example, can trace their lineage back to Western Europe, and they often stem from several different European nationalities. The genealogies of one's family today are expected to provide a direct record with no broken links to the past. (Yet, many who have genealogical records probably cannot provide an endless array of records going back more than three or four centuries.)

Our modern expectations regarding genealogy are much different from what is seen in the Tanach. It is common in the Tanach to see **telescoped genealogies** that purposefully *skip generations* in order for a Biblical author to make an important theological point, or to draw one's attention to the people actually listed.[46] An easy-to-identify example is seen in the genealogy of Ezra the Priest, given to us in both 1 Chronicles 6:3-15 and Ezra 7:1-15:

Genealogy of Ezra the Priest		
1 Chronicles 6:3-15	Ezra 7:1-5	combined
Aaron	Aaron	Aaron
Eleazar	Eleazar	Eleazar
Phinehas	Phinehas	Phinehas
Abishua	Abishua	Abishua
Bukki	Bukki	Bukki
Uzzi	Uzzi	Uzzi
Zerahiah	Zerahiah	Zerahiah
Meraioth	Meraioth	Meraioth
Amariah	Azariah	*Amariah*
Ahitub	Amariah	*Ahitub*
Zadok	Ahitub	*Zadok*
Ahimaaz	Zadok	*Ahimaaz*
Azariah	Shallum	*Azariah*
Johanan	Hilkiah	*Johanan*
Azariah	Azariah	Azariah
Amariah	Seraiah	Amariah
Ahitub		Ahitub
Zadok		Zadok
Shallum		Shallum

---

[46] John Millam (n.d.). *The Genesis Genealogies. Reasons to Believe.* Retrieved 14 October, 2007, from <http://www.reasons.org>.

Hilkiah		Hilkiah
Azariah		Azariah
Seraiah		Seraiah

While doing something like this is completely unacceptable in the modern era, Ezra 7:1-5 *excludes* six people (*italicized* in "combined" column above) from the genealogical list of Ezra the Priest that is seen in 1 Chronicles 6:3-15. Why does the list do this? Obviously, the author of Ezra is communicating something to his audience that the Chronicler is not. The names listed are not just used to establish the credibility of Ezra, but also illustrate his importance by recalling those who have preceded him.

It is very obvious to see that Yeshua's genealogy given in Luke 3 follows a similar pattern, as it traces ancestors from Eli (or Heli in some versions) all the way to Adam (Luke 3:23-38). Luke is telescoping his record, giving his readers the "high points" of Yeshua's lineage, skipping over people in great stride. In stressing a lineage all the way back to Adam, Luke is likely connecting his readers with Yeshua's identification with humanity as a kind of Second Adam.

The real issue in Luke's genealogy involves the immediate person described after "Joseph" in Luke 3:23: "When He began His ministry, Yeshua Himself was about thirty years of age, being, as was supposed, the son of Joseph, the son of Eli." There have been several proposals made by theologians regarding what this might mean, including Luke's genealogy being the actual descent of Joseph, husband of Mary, and Matthew's genealogy being the royal descent. Another suggestion is that Eli and Jacob (Matthew 1:16) were half-brothers, having the same mother but different fathers, and that Eli died and Jacob married his widow, becoming a step-father to Joseph. Still, others propose that the genealogy of Luke 3 is Mary's genealogy, given the remark "as was supposed," as a reference to the virgin birth, yet this is complicated because Mary is not listed by name.

Walter L. Liefield makes the pertinent observation, "we possess not a poverty but a plethora of possibilities. Therefore the lack of certainty due to incomplete information need not imply error...[I]t is not possible to know how Luke would have handled a genealogy involving a virgin birth, and so 'the case is unique.'"[47] Indeed, the principal thrust of Luke's genealogy is that we understand Yeshua's identification with the human race (cf. Philippians 2:5-11). Luke does not open his Gospel with the genealogy of Yeshua, indicating that for his broad audience of both First Century Jews and Greeks and Romans, genealogy would not have been as important to them as some of the other features of Yeshua's identity.

Matthew's genealogy is much more complicated than Luke's, given his largely Jewish audience, as his specific aim is to identify Yeshua as the "son of David, son of Abraham" (Matthew 1:1). Genealogy was very important to the Jews of the First Century. Yeshua is established to be of the royal line of David. But whereas Luke moves backward all the way to Adam, Matthew moves forward from Abraham to David and finally to Yeshua.

The likelihood of telescoping employed in Matthew 1 is also very high, and the rendering of "**A** fathered/was the father of **B**" as seen in many Bible versions (RSV, NASU, NIV, NRSV) **is unfortunate**[48] as the average Bible reader will expect there to be a *direct* father-son-grandson-great-grandson relationship, when in some cases *there is not*. Indeed, as Ancient Near Eastern scholar K.A. Kitchen points out, "The phrase 'A begat B' does not always imply direct parenthood. This is shown by its use in Matthew 1 in cases where links are known (from the Old Testament) to have been omitted."[49] Furthermore, some of the people "inserted" into Matthew's genealogy who do not appear in the Tanach (i.e., Amminadab in Matthew 1:4) need not be a result of "tampering" with the text, but the fact that Matthew is working from genealogical sources that are no longer extant, or that there was an oral tradition in Joseph's family of additional people not seen in 1 Chronicles.[50]

---

[47] Walter L. Liefield, "Luke," in Frank E. Gaebelein, ed. et. al, *Expositor's Bible Commentary* (Grand Rapids: Zondervan, 1984), 8:861-862.

[48] The NKJV uses the more proper formula "**A** begot **B**."

[49] K.A. Kitchen, *Ancient Orient and Old Testament* (Madison, WI: InterVarsity, 1966), pp 38-39.

[50] Cf. Hegg, *Matthew: Chapters 1-7*, pp 20-22; D.A. Carson, "Matthew," in *EXP*, 8:65.

Answering the "Frequently Avoided Questions" About the Messiahship of Yeshua

There are two major issues that are brought forward by anti-missionaries regarding Matthew's genealogy. The first concerns Matthew's listing of King Jeconiah (1:11), and the fact that Jeremiah prophesied that a descendant of his would not sit upon his throne again:

"Thus says the LORD, 'Write this man down childless, a man who will not prosper in his days; for no man of his descendants will prosper sitting on the throne of David or ruling again in Judah'" (Jeremiah 22:30).

Anti-missionaries have been able to disturb many people by claiming that since Matthew lists Jeconiah in Yeshua's genealogical list, then Yeshua cannot rule over Israel since Jeconiah was punished by God. However, an important clue is given to us by Matthew when he writes, "Josiah begot Jeconiah and his brothers **about the time they were carried away to Babylon**" (Matthew 1:11, NKJV). Far from this being a permanent curse upon Jeconiah and the kingly line of Judah, the Talmud indicates that this curse was only to be temporary, with the exile to Babylon being sufficient punishment:

"Said R. Yohanan, 'Exile atones for everything, for it is said, "Thus says the Lord, Write this man childless, a man that shall not prosper in his days, for no man of his seed shall prosper sitting upon the throne of David and ruling any more in Judah" (Jer. 22:30). *After [the king] was exiled, it is written,* 'And the sons of Jechoniah, the same is Assir, Shealtiel, his son ...' (1Ch. 3:17). [So he was not childless, and through exile he had atoned for his sins.]" 'Assir' because his mother conceived in prison" (b.*Sanhedrin* 37b).[51]

Here, we see that the Sages considered the curse issued by Jeremiah against Jeconiah to be lifted as a result of the exile, because he very clearly does have additional descendants (1 Chronicles 3:17), which Jeremiah's prophecy said he would not have. Matthew's insertion of Jeconiah in the genealogy of Yeshua is not invalid.

---

[51] *The Babylonian Talmud: A Translation and Commentary.* MS Windows XP. Peabody, MA: Hendrickson, 2005. CD-ROM.

The second issue anti-missionaries commonly point out regarding Matthew's genealogy concerns his concluding remark, "So all the generations from Abraham to David are fourteen generations; from David to the deportation to Babylon, fourteen generations; and from the deportation to Babylon to the Messiah, fourteen generations" (Matthew 1:17). Obviously, while the fact that Matthew likely does some telescoping is not considered, if one adds the third set of generations from Jeconiah to Joseph (Matthew 1:12-16), we only see thirteen generations.

One possible explanation is that both Joseph and Mary, listed in Matthew 1:16, are intended to be counted as two generations. Another explanation is that Yeshua's own generation is to be counted. Still, a third explanation is that what is really being communicated is the connection to *David* (דְּוִד), a common enough Hebrew word (not necessitating a Hebrew composition for Matthew)[52] whose numerical value is fourteen and could have been easily recognized by Judean or Diaspora Jews.[53]

The fact that Matthew can list names according to a formula of "fourteen," via telescoping and/or referencing *David*, is not uncommon to the Tanach. Two significant genealogies that communicate something similar are the anti-diluvians of Genesis 5 from Adam to Noah, and the post-diluvians of Genesis 11 from Noah to Abraham. Both genealogies list "ten" generations. As Kitchen describes, "there is...symmetry of ten generations before the Flood and ten generations after the Flood. With this, one may compare the three series of fourteen generations in Matthew's genealogy of Christ...which is *known* to be selective, and not wholly continuous."[54] Sarna concurs, "There is reason to believe that the ten-generation pattern for genealogies was favored by Western Semites in general and that the convention left its mark

---

[52] As Hegg, *Matthew: Chapters 1-7*, 15 notes, "Even if Matthew's readers were receiving his words in Greek, they most likely would have been familiar with the Hebrew spelling of the name."

[53] Carson, in *EXP*, 8:69.

This would be one of the few isolated incidents in Scripture where use of gematria is valid, with both a specific name and number referenced.

[54] Kitchen, 37.

on the historiography of Israel."[55] Thus, the number "ten" in the Ancient Near East brought with it an aura of distinction (perhaps royal distinction), designed in Genesis 5 and 11 to give some "high points" of individuals who lived between Adam and Noah, and then Noah and Abraham—but by no means are all of the generations of people between Adam and Noah, and then Noah and Abraham, recorded on these lists.[56]

Properly understanding the genealogies of Matthew 1 and Luke 3 is a definite area where anti-missionaries reveal how they are often not engaged with the Ancient Near Eastern background of the Tanach. And indeed, it is difficult to not subject the Bible to our modern expectations of precision. However, neither Luke in his telescoped genealogy of Yeshua going back to Adam, nor Matthew in his formulated genealogy of 14 generations connected to David, have done something irregular. On the contrary, anti-missionaries have preyed on the ignorance of people, subjecting ancient texts to modern-day expectations of precision, divorcing them from their original context.

False Claim #7
Isaiah 7:14 has been purposefully mistranslated with "virgin" in Christian Bibles, to fit a pagan concept of a virgin giving birth, specifically to Jesus.

Refuting the virgin birth of Yeshua is a common practice of liberals in Christianity, who often doubt anything supernatural, and consequently anti-missionaries have joined the bandwagon by claiming Isaiah 7:14 is not a prophecy of the Messiah to come, that the Gospels have misapplied this word, and even that the

---

[55] Nahum M. Sarna, *JPS Torah Commentary: Genesis* (Philadelphia: Jewish Publication Society, 1989), 40; cf. Duane A. Garrett, ed., et. al., *NIV Archaeological Study Bible* (Grand Rapids: Zondervan, 2005), 12.

[56] Kitchen's concluding remark, "one cannot use these genealogies to fix the date of the Flood or of earliest Man" (p 39) asks questions that today's Messianic movement is largely unprepared to answer, as it still relies quite heavily on the conclusions of Seventeenth Century Archbishop James Ussher.

Cf. R.K. Harrison, "Chronology from Adam to Abraham," in *Introduction to the Old Testament* (Grand Rapids: Eerdmans, 1969), pp 147-163. Also consult the FAQ entries on the TNN website, "Genesis 5, 11 Genealogies" and "6,000 Year Teaching."

concept of a virgin giving birth is "pagan." Messianics who are unfamiliar with the Isaianic expectation of one to be born find themselves very easy to be manipulated.

It is undeniable that Isaiah 7:14 plays a role in the Messianic expectation of the Apostolic Scriptures. Matthew 1:22-23 attests, "Now all this took place to fulfill what was spoken by the Lord through the prophet: 'BEHOLD, THE VIRGIN SHALL BE WITH CHILD AND SHALL BEAR A SON, AND THEY SHALL CALL HIS NAME IMMANUEL,' which translated means, 'GOD WITH US.'" Here as a prophetic support for Yeshua's Messiahship and Incarnation, Isaiah 7:14 is quoted. When the Revised Standard Version was originally published in 1952, it caused quite a stir rendering Isaiah 7:14 as "Behold, a young woman shall conceive and bear a son, and shall call his name Immanuel." Consequently, since then, the subject of the virgin birth and how Isaiah 7:14 should be viewed has been quite a debate.[57]

The original backdrop of this word concerns an alliance between Rezin, king of Aram (Syria), and Pekah, king of the Northern Kingdom of Ephraim, who prepare to attack the Southern Kingdom of Judah (Isaiah 7:1-2). If this alliance is successful, and Judah is destroyed, so is all hope of God being faithful to His covenant promises. The Prophet Isaiah and his son Shear-Jashub are directed by God to go to King Ahaz of Judah (Isaiah 7:3-6), and he is to be specifically told, "It shall not stand nor shall it come to pass" (Isaiah 7:7). Isaiah asks Ahaz to request of God a sign that He will be faithful to His promises, and although Ahaz refuses (Isaiah 7:12), the Prophet tells him what the sign will be:

"And he said, 'Hear then, O house of David! Is it too little for you to weary men, that you weary my God also? Therefore the Lord himself will give you a sign. Behold, a young woman shall conceive and bear a son, and shall call his name Immanuel.' He shall eat curds and honey when he knows how to refuse the evil and choose the good" (Isaiah 7:13-15, RSV).

---

[57] For a summary of this debate, consult "Virgin Birth of Christ," in *Baker Encyclopedia of Christian Apologetics*, pp 759-764.

It is at this point that the anti-missionaries stop. Matthew is stated by them to have misapplied a word that was given to King Ahaz in ancient times, which only speaks of the conception of a child called Immanuel. People are then easily led to conclude that the whole "Christian" idea of a so-called virgin birth is wrong.

First to take notice of is the first clause in Isaiah 7:14: *yitten Adonai hu l'khem ot* (יִתֵּן אֲדֹנָי הוּא לָכֶם אוֹת), literally "will give the Lord Him to you a sign." The most overlooked part of this clause is how *l'khem* or "to you" appears in the **plural**, not the singular,[58] thus indicating that the sign of which Isaiah speaks regards the entire House of David, and not just King Ahaz as an individual.

The second clause indicates what is going to happen: *hinneh ha'almah hara v'yoledet ben* (הִנֵּה הָעַלְמָה הָרָה וְיֹלֶדֶת בֵּן), literally "behold the young woman/virgin look and bearing a son." There is endless controversy as to how *ha'almah* (הָעַלְמָה), either "the young woman/maiden" or "the virgin," should be translated. Note that it is insufficient for us to just consider *almah* here; the definite article "the" in *ha'almah* is what is used in the text, and is intensified by being prefixed with the imperative *hinneh* or "behold."

Is the scope of Isaiah's prophecy here just limited to a young woman conceiving and having a child? Indeed, the most common anti-missionary tactic is to say that if Isaiah were truly speaking of a virgin, then the word *betulah* (בְּתוּלָה), used to describe Rebekah in Genesis 24:16, would have been used. However, when one examines varied Tanach usages of the word *almah* and weigh them into the equation, this is not the conclusion that a responsible interpreter can draw.

It is very true that Rebekah is described as a *betulah* or "virgin" in Genesis 24:16, but later in Genesis 24:43, as an unmarried woman, she is also called an *almah*. The usage of *betulah* is unclear, necessitating the addition of the clause "no man had had relations with her" in Genesis 24:16, whereas the usage of *almah* requires no such clarification. Miriam, the sister of

---

[58] The LXX follows suit, rendering *l'khem* with the plural *humin* (ὑμῖν).

- 127 -

Moses, is referred to as an *almah* in Exodus 2:8, being called by the daughter of Pharaoh to fetch Moses' mother to nurse him, and we should surely not expect for Miriam to have had sexual relations at such a young age.

The pre-Christian Septuagint translators undoubtedly understood the difference between *betulah* and *almah,* and thus they were able to render *almah* as *parthenos* (παρθένος), "female of marriageable age w. focus on virginity" (*BDAG*).[59] Has Matthew misapplied Isaiah 7:14? It is notable, as it concerns Yeshua's conception, that Mary does say "How can this be, since I do not know a man[60]?" (Luke 1:34, NKJV). Matthew's Gospel, employing the term *parthenos* as the LXX rendered Isaiah 7:14, has made a value judgment. Likewise, so have any Bible translators who have rendered *almah* as "virgin."

This is only part of the issue, though. Has Matthew totally missed the point of the promise to King Ahaz? We need not disconnect Isaiah 7:14 from the verses following in Isaiah 7:16-17:

"For before the boy will know *enough* to refuse evil and choose good, the land whose two kings you dread will be forsaken. The LORD will bring on you, on your people, and on your father's house such days as have never come since the day that Ephraim separated from Judah, the king of Assyria."

Who is this child being talked about? Is this the child who was to be born to the virgin? It cannot go unnoticed that while the plural "you" appears in Isaiah 7:14, *l'khem,* that Isaiah 7:16 says *ha'adamah asher atah qatz m'pn'ei shnei malkeiyha* (שְׁנֵי מְלָכֶיהָ הָאֲדָמָה אֲשֶׁר אַתָּה קָץ מִפְּנֵי), with the singular "you," *atah,* appearing instead. Previously, the dilemma of the House of David as a whole has been described, whereas here the more immediate problem of the Southern Kingdom for its leader, King Ahaz, is in view.

Many readers of Isaiah 7 have thought that there is a kind of dual reference here. A child born during the reign of King Ahaz of the Southern Kingdom would not live very long before the immediate problem threatening Judah, although with some

[59] *BDAG*, 777.
[60] Grk. *andra ou ginōskō* (ἄνδρα οὐ γινώσκω).

- 128 -

negative aftermath, would be gone. Partial fulfillment of Isaiah 7 would lead to a greater degree of fulfillment in later history, via the virgin birth of Yeshua the Messiah.[61]

Another thought is seen in how Hegg suggests that the usage of *na'ar* (נַעַר) or "lad" in Isaiah 7:16 is to be taken in a generic, somewhat proverbial sense. He indicates, "In a short time (illustrated by the time it takes for a child to grow into moral awareness) the land which the two kings...who had allied together against Jerusalem were fighting for would be forsaken, that is, laid waste."[62] From this perspective, the lad spoken of in vs. 16-17, is not to be viewed as the Messiah to come, but rather is an allusion to the fact that before a period of about twelve years (cf. Deuteronomy 1:39) has expired, King Ahaz' enemies will be dealt with.

This is a good enough proposal, but it has not taken into consideration why *ha'na'ar* (הַנַּעַר) or "the lad/boy," with the definite article, is what appears in Isaiah 7:16, which would need to refer to some specific person. Is this specific lad or boy, the child to be born who would be known as Immanuel? An excellent answer is provided by Michael Rydelnik, in that the boy being referred to in Isaiah 7:16 is actually Isaiah's young son Shear-Jashub, who accompanied the Prophet to witness what was said to King Ahaz. He eloquently addresses some of the difficulties seen in Isaiah 7:13-16:

> "While many have considered v. 16 to be a continuation of the prophecy in 7:13-15, the grammar of the passage suggests otherwise. The opening phrase in Hebrew [*ki b'terem*, כִּי בְּטֶרֶם] can reflect an adversative nuance, allowing for a disjunction between the child described in 7:13-15 and the one described in verse 16. There is a different child in view in this verse.
>
> "*The Identity of the Child.* So who is the child in 7:16? In light of Isaiah being directed to bring his own son to the confrontation with the king at the conduit of the upper pool (cf. 7:3), it makes most sense to identify the lad as Shear-

[61] Cf. Kaiser, *The Messiah in the Old Testament*, pp 160-162; Brown, *Answering Jewish Objections to Jesus, Volume 3*, pp 25-28.

[62] Hegg, *Messiah in the Tanach*, 93.

Jashub. Otherwise there would be no purpose for God directing Isaiah to bring the boy. Thus having promised the virgin birth of the Messiah (7:13-15), the prophet then points to the very small boy that he has brought along and says, 'But before *this* lad (using the article with a demonstrative force) knows enough to refuse evil and choose good, the land whose two kings you dread will be forsaken.' In this way, Shear-Jashub functioned as a sign to the king. Apparently, Isaiah could tell Judah in the very next chapter, 'Here I am with the children the LORD has given me to be signs and wonders in Israel from the LORD of Hosts who dwells on Mount Zion' (8:18).

"*The Identity of the Addressee.* To whom does Isaiah make this prediction? What is not evident in the English text is plain in the Hebrew. The prophet returned to using the second-person singular pronoun in 7:16 ('the land of the two kings *you* [sg.] dread'). In 7:10-11 he used the singular to address King Ahaz. Then, when addressing the house of David with the prophecy of Messiah, he shifted to the plural. But in 7:16, he addressed King Ahaz, using the singular pronoun once again and giving him a near prophecy: before Shear-Jashub would be able to discern good from evil, the northern confederacy attacking Judah would fail. Within two years, Tiglath-Pileser defeated both Israel and Syria, just as the prophet had predicted.

"Having completed his long-term prophecy, Isaiah gave a short-term prophecy. In doing so, he followed a frequent pattern of his book. He consistently did this so his readership could have confidence in the distant prediction by observing the fulfillment in the near one."[63]

Ultimately, the answer that the House of David and King Ahaz would have sought to all the problems of Judah, Israel, and even the nations at large—was only to be found in the far future by a miraculous birth of one who called "Immanuel" or God with us. This is a Child who would live in a time when there would be "curds and honey" (Isaiah 7:15) present, which Rydelnik takes to represent "the food of oppression" (cf. Isaiah 7:21-22), in that "the prophecy of Messiah concludes with a hint

---

[63] Michael Rydelnik, *The Messianic Hope: Is the Hebrew Bible Messianic?* (Nashville: B&H Publishing Group, 2010), pp 157-158.

that He will be born and grow up…at a time when Judah is oppressed by a foreign power,"[64] which would surely be the case with Judea dominated by Rome in the First Century. The One prophesied to be born is a different kind of king who has never before been seen. Indeed, as Isaiah 9:6-7 further describes,

"For a child will be born to us, a son will be given to us; and the government will rest on His shoulders; and His name will be called Wonderful Counselor, Mighty God, Eternal Father, Prince of Peace. There will be no end to the increase of *His* government or of peace, on the throne of David and over his kingdom, to establish it and to uphold it with justice and righteousness from then on and forevermore. The zeal of the LORD of hosts will accomplish this."

For Matthew, Isaiah 7:14 clearly spoke of the Messiah to come, and the text can certainly be understood from this point of view. Indeed, many passages that appear throughout Isaiah 7:1-12:6 can only be applied to a figure to come, including: the wonderful ruling son (Isaiah 9:1-7) and the reign of Jesse's son (Isaiah 11:1-16), **not** someone from Ahaz' contemporary period. Michael L. Brown concludes, "as Matthew looked back at these prophecies hundreds of years later, it would have been apparent to him that (1) these chapters were clearly linked together, and (2) the promises of a worldwide, glorious reign of the promised Davidic king were not yet realized."[65] Isaiah 7:14, as applied to the birth of Yeshua, would not have been provided isolated from other Isaianic expectations considered by Matthew.

The second criticism from anti-missionaries is that the virgin birth—perhaps more correctly termed, at times, the virgin conception—is "pagan." This line of reasoning used to attack the Messiahship of Yeshua can find many who are eager to embrace it, primarily because of the influence of certain "Messianic"

---

[64] Ibid., 156.

His specific reason for this is that "fields will not be cultivated and [they] will become pastures for oxen and sheep (7:23-25). The effect of this will be an overabundance of daily (or butter/curds) because of the pasturing of livestock, and an excess of honey because bees will be able to pollinate the wild flowers" (Ibid.). Assyria is said to have shaved the land of people (Isaiah 7:20), and a similar situation would be in place at the arrival of the Messiah during the Roman era.

[65] Brown, *Answering Jewish Objections to Jesus, Volume 3,* 25.

publications and ministries who during the past decade (1996-present) have directed a great deal of spiritual venom against the Christian Church. It has been widely asserted by these publications and ministries that the Christian Church is "totally saturated" with paganism (and often *their* subjective views of paganism at that). Rather than choose a constructive way to dialogue with Christians about issues such as Torah observance and the Hebraic background of Yeshua's life, in a quest to be Biblical, damning all Christians and the Church is the method that is preferred. So, we should not be surprised when all the rhetoric regarding "paganism" is unleashed that anti-missionaries find a great opportunity to attack a significant area of Apostolic doctrine.

It is not impossible to find some possible parallels between a virgin conceiving by supernatural means, as depicted in the Gospels, and what one sees in pagan mythology. In fact, significant parallels exist between the crucifixion and resurrection of Yeshua and the play Promethus Bound by Aeschylus. If a misguided person wants to use these criteria to reject the Messiahship of Yeshua, and indeed the gospel, one can choose to do so. But I would severely warn the person who takes this course of action **to be consistent in what he or she rejects** on the basis of "paganism"—something that anti-missionaries *fail* to do.

If the virgin conception of Yeshua is indeed "pagan," then could it not also be true that the Creation account and Noahdic Flood are likewise borrowed from paganism? The Sumerian Epic of Gilgamesh strongly mirrors the story of the Flood described in the Bible. How do we know that the Epic of Gilgamesh is not a prototype for what is described in the opening chapters of Genesis?[66] Anti-missionaries are certainly not going to answer these questions, yet they are perfectly valid because liberals who deny Yeshua's virgin birth likewise deny that the opening chapters of the Bible, the Exodus, the Conquest, and possibly even the monarchy of Israel is not valid history and is largely

---

[66] Cf. Jon D. Levenson, "Genesis," in Adele Berlin and Marc Zvi Brettler, eds., *The Jewish Study Bible* (Oxford: Oxford University Press, 2004), pp 8-11.

mythology. How far are we willing to go? Will one be consistent with how much of the Bible could in actuality be "pagan"? Or, will one have the discernment to see that the enemy has always had a counterfeit to God's truth?[67]

False Claim #8
Matthew 27:9 has deliberately misreferenced the Tanach. The text says that "Jeremiah" spoke a prophecy that should really be a word credited to Zechariah.

At this point, when the naïve and spiritually immature person has been lulled to accept the largely disengaged, and overly simplistic perspective of the anti-missionary, hearing that Matthew 27:9 has misreferenced a Tanach passage will often be accepted without any serious examination or consideration. Interestingly enough, this is one of the easiest claims against Yeshua's Messiahship that can be responded to.

Matthew 27:9 says, "Then that which was spoken through Jeremiah the prophet was fulfilled: 'AND THEY TOOK THE THIRTY PIECES OF SILVER, THE PRICE OF THE ONE WHOSE PRICE HAD BEEN SET by the sons of Israel.'" David H. Stern points out the possibility, "the scroll of the Prophets may have originally begun with Jeremiah…not Isaiah; if so, Mattityahu [Matthew] by naming Jeremiah is referring to the Prophets as a group, not naming the particular prophet quoted"[68] (cf. b.*Bava Batra* 14b-15a). Likewise to be considered is the fact that two likely Scripture passages are being melded together: Jeremiah 32:6-9 and Zechariah 11:12-13:[69]

> "And Jeremiah said, 'The word of the LORD came to me, saying, "Behold, Hanamel the son of Shallum your uncle is coming to you, saying, 'Buy for yourself my field which is at Anathoth, for you have the right of redemption to buy *it*.'"' Then Hanamel my uncle's son came to me in the court of the guard according to the word of the LORD and said to me, "Buy my field, please, that is at Anathoth, which is in the land of Benjamin; for you have the right of possession and

---

[67] For a further discussion, consult the author's article, "Is the Story of Yeshua Pagan?"

[68] Stern, *Jewish New Testament Commentary*, 83.

[69] Aland, *GNT*, 108.

> the redemption is yours; buy *it* for yourself." Then I knew that this was the word of the LORD. I bought the field which was at Anathoth from Hanamel my uncle's son, and I weighed out the silver for him, seventeen shekels of silver'" (Jeremiah 32:6-9).

> "I said to them, 'If it is good in your sight, give *me* my wages; but if not, never mind!' So they weighed out thirty *shekels* of silver as my wages. Then the LORD said to me, 'Throw it to the potter, *that* magnificent price at which I was valued by them.' So I took the thirty *shekels* of silver and threw them to the potter in the house of the LORD" (Zechariah 11:12-13).

Of the two passages quoted, Zechariah 11:12-13 is clearly the one that is more probably referred to by Matthew in relation to the field purchased with the blood money given to Judas Iscariot. Zechariah 11 speaks of the shepherd in God's flock whose job it was to help separate the condemned sheep and the ones who are to be shown His grace (Zechariah 11:7-9). Judas Iscariot certainly played in this role via his betrayal of Yeshua, thus resulting in His execution. Only with Judas' betrayal could the plan of God be fully enacted.

Yet, Jeremiah's name is probably mentioned by Matthew to draw attention to the fact that just as Jeremiah was directed by God to purchase the field of Hanamel, so would the blood money given to Judas for betraying Yeshua at least be directed for some positive task, not going to total waste. Likewise, just as Jeremiah was directed by God to do something, so does Matthew's quotation point out something that God is ultimately responsible for. It would be very easy for one to think that Yeshua's execution was solely the work of evil people, when in fact it was part of God's Divine plan to accomplish the redemption of the world.

Applying Scripture passages in this manner is not unique to the Gospels. Mark (1:2-3) similarly quotes Malachi 3:1 and Isaiah 40:3, yet makes a reference to Isaiah as the better-known prophet.

Sadly, anti-missionaries are not going to take the time to consider the possible theological ideas being communicated among several prophecies meshed together, instead preferring an overly-simplistic approach.

False Claim #9
The suffering servant of Isaiah 53 is Israel, not Jesus.

Isaiah 53 is indeed a very controversial passage of Scripture when it comes to the Messiahship of Yeshua and the exact identity of the servant described. There are multiple views that have been extant in Judaism, including: identifying the servant as the people of Israel and their role in history, the Prophet Jeremiah and his suffering, or perhaps even Moses.[70] Christian interpreters have almost always associated the servant of Isaiah 53 with Yeshua the Messiah, and indeed, the Apostolic Scriptures appropriate verses from Isaiah 53 and directly apply them to Yeshua (Isaiah 53:1 and John 12:32, Romans 10:16; Isaiah 53:4 and Matthew 8:17; Isaiah 53:6 and 1 Peter 2:25; Isaiah 53:9 and 1 Peter 2:22; Isaiah 53:12 and Luke 22:37), not to mention all of the other typological connections that parallel events in the ministry of Yeshua. We would all do well to (re)familiarize ourselves with the words of Isaiah 53:

> "Who has believed our message? And to whom has the arm of the LORD been revealed? For He grew up before Him like a tender shoot, and like a root out of parched ground; He has no *stately* form or majesty that we should look upon Him, nor appearance that we should be attracted to Him. He was despised and forsaken of men, a man of sorrows and acquainted with grief; and like one from whom men hide their face He was despised, and we did not esteem Him. Surely our griefs He Himself bore, and our sorrows He carried; yet we ourselves esteemed Him stricken, smitten of God, and afflicted. But He was pierced through for our transgressions, He was crushed for our iniquities; the chastening for our well-being *fell* upon Him, and by His scourging we are healed. All of us like sheep have gone astray, each of us has turned to his own way; but the LORD has caused the iniquity of us all to fall on Him. He was oppressed and He was afflicted, yet He did not open His

---

[70] Benjamin D. Sommer, "Isaiah," in *Jewish Study Bible*, 891.

mouth; like a lamb that is led to slaughter, and like a sheep that is silent before its shearers, so He did not open His mouth. By oppression and judgment He was taken away; and as for His generation, who considered that He was cut off out of the land of the living for the transgression of my people, to whom the stroke *was due*? His grave was assigned with wicked men, yet He was with a rich man in His death, because He had done no violence, nor was there any deceit in His mouth. But the LORD was pleased to crush Him, putting *Him* to grief; if He would render Himself *as* a guilt offering, He will see *His* offspring, He will prolong *His* days, and the good pleasure of the LORD will prosper in His hand. As a result of the anguish of His soul, He will see *it and* be satisfied; by His knowledge the Righteous One, My Servant, will justify the many, as He will bear their iniquities. Therefore, I will allot Him a portion with the great, and He will divide the booty with the strong; because He poured out Himself to death, and was numbered with the transgressors; yet He Himself bore the sin of many, and interceded for the transgressors."

All of us at one point or another have probably heard these words recited, or possibly delivered via Handel's operatic performance *The Messiah*. There are an extreme amount of parallels between these verses and the account of Yeshua that are not difficult to see, if one possesses a cursory knowledge of the Apostolic Scriptures:

- The origins of Yeshua in the Gospels are described as being very humble (Isaiah 53:2), and how no one followed Him because of His appearance.
- The Gospels describe how Yeshua was not always accepted, and indeed was frequently despised (Isaiah 53:3).
- Yeshua had a healing ministry, bearing the infirmities of others (Isaiah 53:4).
- Yeshua is portrayed in the Gospels as bearing the sins of the world (Isaiah 53:5-6).
- Yeshua underwent extreme pain and torture prior to His crucifixion (Isaiah 53:7), remaining

silent before His accusers (Matthew 27:12-14; Mark 14:60-61; 15:4-5; Luke 23:8-9; John 19:8-9).

- Yeshua is attested in the Gospels to have had an unfair trial (Isaiah 53:8).

- Yeshua was executed as a common criminal, yet was buried in a rich man's, Joseph of Arimathea's, tomb (Isaiah 53:9-10; cf. Matthew 27:57-60).

- As a result of Yeshua's life, the Apostolic Scriptures attest that human beings can be fully justified or declared righteous (Isaiah 53:11).

- The Apostolic Scriptures attest that Yeshua is the mediator between God the Father and humanity (Isaiah 53:12).

There have been many excellent, thorough studies conducted on the meaning of these words, and how they are undoubtedly connected to Yeshua, His ministry, and His atoning work for the world as portrayed in the Apostolic Scriptures that I recommend you consult.[71] It is because of these many connections between Isaiah 53 and the ministry of Yeshua that, as the *Jewish Study Bible* notes, "Medieval rabbinic commentators devoted considerable attention to refuting this interpretation."[72] Indeed, of all the potential Messianic prophecies in the Tanach, it is Isaiah 53 where the most attention has been spent.

What disturbs many Messianic Believers is when they hear that Judaism has not interpreted this passage in a framework relating to the Messiah to come. Some easily brush this reason aside as being reactionary on Judaism's part, with the Synagogue not conducting any serious examination or consideration for what is being said by Isaiah when compared to the ministry and service of Yeshua. But, people, who are either unsure of Yeshua's Messiahship, or perhaps give too much credence to "the Rabbis" in their Biblical examination, can be often convinced that Yeshua is not the Messiah when they hear the line that "Judaism

---

[71] I specifically refer the reader to Kaiser, *The Messiah in the Old Testament*, pp 178-181; Hegg, *The Messiah in the Tanach*, pp 109-121; and Brown, *Answering Jewish Objections to Jesus, Volume 3*, pp 49-86.

[72] Sommer, in *Jewish Study Bible*, 891.

interprets Isaiah 53 as a reference to Israel, not the Messiah." Actual examination and consideration for the meaning of the text is often not given, and the non-Jewish person wanting to convert to Judaism, or the Messianic Jew wanting to return to the Synagogue, now feels justified in doing so.

No one can deny the fact that Isaiah 53 has been interpreted by Jews in the past as relating to Israel as the servant of God, and not a suffering Messiah. Certainly, we could expect to see variance among Jewish interpreters before the First Century, some of whom may have not applied Isaiah 53 to a singular figure, although there are certainly ancient interpretations that clearly do apply it to a single figure. Following the times of Yeshua, historical Jewish interpreters such as Rashi, Ibn Ezra, and Radak applied the text to Israel, yet there was also variance, as some in the later Chassidic movement sought to apply Isaiah 53 to Menachem Schneerson.[73] Anti-missionaries are not going to be objective with the Jewish history of interpretation of Isaiah 53, presenting you with all of the options that are available and have been proposed. Brown summarizes this dilemma:

"...[W]hen you realize that sections from Isaiah 52:12-53:12 are quoted several times in the New Testament, and the passage as a whole can arguably be called *the* clearest prophecy of Jesus in the entire Tanakh....many traditional Jewish commentators and teachers have *still* interpreted the prophecy as Messianic. How tempting it would have been for the Talmudic rabbis and their successors to interpret this passage with reference to Israel—rather than to the Messiah or any other individual— seeing that it played such an important role in Christian interpretation and polemics. Yet they did not interpret the passage with reference to the nation of Israel in any recorded traditional source for almost one thousand years, nor did they interpret it with reference to national Israel with unanimity thereafter."[74]

Indeed, the bulk of Rabbinic interpretation regarding Isaiah 53 as Israel, and not a Messianic figure or single individual, came

---

[73] Brown, *Answering Jewish Objections of Jesus, Volume 3,* pp 49-50.

[74] Ibid., 50.

during the Middle Ages long after the ministry of Yeshua. If one is going to truly consider Jewish interpretations of Isaiah 53, then a person needs to take a few steps back and look at a much broader array of Jewish interpretations that have existed over the millennia. When we do this, **the key issue that needs to be considered is whether or not the Apostolic Scriptures or New Testament can serve as a definitively *Jewish witness* in the discussion.** Were the Apostolic writers misled in their interpretation, or did they have as much to contribute as any Jewish person in the First Century? Were the Apostles wrong to apply the prophecies of Isaiah to what they saw in the ministry and service of Yeshua of Nazareth? I can only answer for myself: I do not believe the Apostles were misled when they saw Yeshua as the epitome of what Isaiah 53 prophesied.[75]

False Claim #10
Human sacrifice is deplorable to God. How can Jesus be "the sacrifice" for all humanity when God Himself would never accept it?

The final disturbing claim that is made against the Messiahship of Yeshua is directed against His crucifixion. The overwhelming conclusion of the Apostolic Scriptures is that Yeshua died to atone for the sins of all humanity. As the Apostle Paul summarizes it, "For I delivered to you as of first importance what I also received, that Messiah died for our sins according to the Scriptures, and that He was buried, and that He was raised on the third day according to the Scriptures" (1 Corinthians 15:3-4). Indeed, the purpose of celebrating Passover as Believers is so that we might "proclaim the Lord's death until He comes" (1 Corinthians 11:26). Yeshua's death and subsequent resurrection are the cornerstones of our faith, something that the Apostles believed was embodied in the message of the Tanach.

Many liberal Christian theologians certainly doubt that Yeshua was physically resurrected from the dead, and so denying anything supernatural they propose that the Disciples

---

[75] For a further discussion, consult the author's entry for the Book of Isaiah in *A Survey of the Tanach for the Practical Messianic*.

simply hallucinated His resurrection. On the other side of this argument Messianics encounter anti-missionaries who claim that a human sacrifice would never be accepted by God. Both issues: hallucinating Yeshua's resurrection, and an unacceptable sacrifice, are more *ideological* than they are theological. One presupposes that supernatural events cannot take place, and the other presupposes that there is no precedent in Scripture for people being sacrificed before God. Both rely on shock value.

There is, in fact, very clear precedent in the Tanach for people being offered as sacrifices before God. God very plainly asked Abraham, "Take your son, your favored one, Isaac, whom you love, and go to the land of Moriah, and offer him there as a burnt offering on one of the heights that I will point out to you" (Genesis 22:2, NJPS). Indeed, the narrative tells us that not only did Abraham obey the Lord, but Isaac went willingly:

"Abraham took the wood of the burnt offering and laid it on Isaac his son, and he took in his hand the fire and the knife. So the two of them walked on together. Isaac spoke to Abraham his father and said, 'My father!' And he said, 'Here I am, my son.' And he said, 'Behold, the fire and the wood, but where is the lamb for the burnt offering?' Abraham said, 'God will provide for Himself the lamb for the burnt offering, my son.' So the two of them walked on together" (Genesis 22:6-8).

Abraham responds to Isaac's question about the sacrifice with the words, "God will provide for Himself the lamb for the burnt offering," somewhat darting around the question. While some would stop there, indicating that Abraham expected just a lamb (Heb. *seh*, שֶׂה) to be provided, and Isaac is accompanying his father on an interesting journey, the following actions when Abraham and Isaac arrive at the designated place speak for themselves:

"Then they came to the place of which God had told him; and Abraham built the altar there and arranged the wood, and bound his son Isaac and laid him on the altar, on top of the wood. Abraham stretched out his hand and took the knife to slay his son" (Genesis 22:9-10).

The Hebrew verb *shachat* (שָׁחַט), appearing in the Qal stem (simple action, active voice), clearly means "to slaughter, kill"

(*HALOT*).[76] We see that Abraham had every intention of taking his knife and terminating the life of his son as a sacrifice before the Almighty, just as He had asked him to do. Yet, just at the moment when Abraham is ready to kill Isaac, he is stopped:

"But the angel of the LORD called to him from heaven and said, 'Abraham, Abraham!' And he said, 'Here I am.' He said, 'Do not stretch out your hand against the lad, and do nothing to him; for now I know that you fear God, since you have not withheld your son, your only son, from Me'" (Genesis 22:11-12).

Abraham is told that he has fulfilled the request that God had of him. Abraham has not "withheld your son, your favored one, from Me" (NJPS). Abraham, being committed in his mind to kill Isaac and present him as a burnt offering, goes as far as preparing to kill him. But rather than his son being killed, we see that "a ram caught in the thicket by his horns" (Genesis 22:13) is what is offered before the Lord. The author of Hebrews appropriates this scene, considering it to be a foreshadowing of the sacrifice Yeshua would make as the Son of God:

"By faith Abraham, when he was tested, offered up Isaac, and he who had received the promises was offering up his only begotten *son*; *it was he* to whom it was said, 'IN ISAAC YOUR DESCENDANTS SHALL BE CALLED' [Genesis 21:12]. He considered that God is able to raise *people* even from the dead, **from which he also received him back as a type**" (Hebrews 11:17-19).

The typology of Isaac's binding, or the *Aqedah* (עֲקֵדָה) as it is commonly called in Jewish theology, is what is offered as valid evidence of Yeshua's sacrifice. This kind of sacrifice, with definite precedent in the Torah, is what is ultimately realized via Yeshua's atonement. Yeshua is portrayed in the Gospels as being the only, beloved Son of God (John 3:16) whose sacrifice will atone for the sins of all humanity. Whereas Isaac did *not* go "all the way" in being killed, Yeshua on the other hand, *was killed*.

The sacrifice of Yeshua at Golgotha (Calvary) is to be contrasted against prohibitions in the Torah forbidding child sacrifice to Canaanite gods such as Molech (Leviticus 18:21; 20:2-5; 2 Kings 23:10; Jeremiah 32:35). Indeed, Solomon is attested in

---

[76] *HALOT*, 2:1458.

the Biblical record as having built temples to Molech (1 Kings 11:7), and actual human sacrifice probably took place in sectors of the Southern Kingdom all the way until the Babylonian exile.[77] Knowing the dire consequences of what resulted to Israel because of such heinous sin, it is ludicrous to think that the Apostles see Yeshua's sacrifice before God in a similar light. Even more ridiculous is to think that Yeshua's sacrifice before God would be like the temporary sacrifice appeasing a pagan deity like Molech. On the contrary, as the Apostle Paul describes it, Yeshua's sacrifice is unique because it covers the sins of both the righteous and unrighteous:

"For while we were still helpless, at the right time Messiah died for the ungodly. For one will hardly die for a righteous man; though perhaps for the good man someone would dare even to die. But God demonstrates His own love toward us, in that while we were yet sinners, Messiah died for us" (Romans 5:6-8).

If anything, Yeshua is portrayed as being the substitute for the common death penalty that all human beings since Adam fall under as sinners in rebellion toward God. This is not "human sacrifice"; it is Yeshua, God's Son, being the substitute penalty for all of us. And Yeshua, by His very sacrifice, has absorbed onto Himself the capital punishment of the Torah (Colossians 2:14).[78] This is a far cry from the human sacrifice seen in the Ancient Near East.

The Torah does make it clear that the Israelites were prohibited from sacrificing people the way that their Canaanite neighbors often did. Such acts were considered to be an abomination to the Lord. But, the Torah likewise portrays Abraham being asked by God to sacrifice his only son to Him. **This is what portrays the ultimate presentation of God's Son before Him as a sacrifice to atone for the sins of all humanity.**

---

[77] Cf. J. Gray, "Molech, Moloch," in George Buttrick, ed. et. al., *The Interpreter's Dictionary of the Bible*, 4 vols. (Nashville: Abingdon, 1962), 3:422-423.

[78] For some useful discussion, consult the article "The Significance of the Messiah Event" by Margaret McKee Huey and J.K. McKee, appearing in the *Messianic Torah Helper* (forthcoming).

The Criticism Only Messianics Can Respond To

Many of the reasons that are used by anti-missionaries as proofs against Yeshua's Messiahship, as we have just seen, can usually be easily responded to because anti-missionaries over-simplify the meaning of verses, and they are largely deficient because they fail to take into account the context, historical background, and larger scope of a passage. Both Christian and Messianic interpreters have shown most anti-missionary claims to be quite misguided and incomplete (and the only ones not shown as such are the claims we cannot predict). However, there is one significant claim against Yeshua's Messiahship that only Messianics can really respond to:

Jesus Christ came to abolish the Torah of Moses

Current Christian positions regarding the role of the Torah do indeed vary. Many rightly see that the Torah or Law of Moses plays a role, albeit limited, in one's faith experience with God. They see that the "moral law" contained in the Torah is continuous, and that God certainly expects us to be good, upstanding people. They rightly recognize that the Torah's principal commandments are to love God and neighbor (Deuteronomy 6:5; Leviticus 19:18), concepts fully reemphasized by Jesus (Matthew 22:35-37; Mark 12:28-31; Luke 10:25-28).

Others, however, believe that via His sacrifice on the cross that Yeshua the Messiah abolished the Torah in its entirety— meaning that its commandments relating to not only Israel as a national people (i.e., practices such as the Sabbath, appointed times, kosher laws, circumcision) have been abolished—but also those relating to morality. Some espouse that "the law of Christ" (Galatians 6:2) is actually a different set of instruction, divorced from the Torah, and that all the Law of Moses could do was to place people in bondage.

It is this latter group that often draws the most attention by anti-missionaries, *and is often the principal reason why Jews reject the Messiahship of Yeshua*, precisely because the Messianic expectation of the Prophets is that the Messiah will come to uphold the Torah as a standard of God's righteousness. Consider this basic Messianic prophecy with which most Christians are familiar:

"Now it will come about that in the last days the mountain of the house of the LORD will be established as the chief of the mountains, and will be raised above the hills; and all the nations will stream to it. And many peoples will come and say, 'Come, let us go up to the mountain of the LORD, to the house of the God of Jacob; that He may teach us concerning His ways and that we may walk in His paths.' For the law will go forth from Zion and the word of the LORD from Jerusalem. And He will judge between the nations, and will render decisions for many peoples; and they will hammer their swords into plowshares and their spears into pruning hooks. Nation will not lift up sword against nation, and never again will they learn war" (Isaiah 2:3; cf. Micah 4:1-3).

Contrary to the Messiah coming to abolish the Torah, or even that observing the Torah as a born again Believer is some kind of "apostasy" against Him, the Messiah is to uphold the standard of the Torah for God's people. It is very true that with Yeshua's arrival and sacrifice, things regarding the Levitical priesthood and animal sacrifices have changed (Hebrews 7:12), capital punishment has largely been nullified (Colossians 2:14), and that the Abrahamic promise of His descendants being a blessing to all nations can be fully realized (Genesis 12:2-3; cf. Galatians 3:8-9). But is this to suggest a widescale abandonment of the morality and ethos of the Torah as many Christian theologians may imply? Is the Torah only good for knowing about the history of the Bible, *not* providing any valid, relevant spiritual instruction today? As Yeshua is so commonly quoted as saying by Messianics,

"Do not think that I came to abolish the Law or the Prophets; I did not come to abolish but to fulfill. For truly I say to you, until heaven and earth pass away, not the smallest letter or stroke shall pass from the Law until all is accomplished. Whoever then annuls one of the least of these commandments, and teaches others *to do* the same, shall be called least in the kingdom of heaven; but whoever keeps and teaches *them*, he shall be called great in the kingdom of heaven" (Matthew 5:17-19).

Unfortunately, many people in today's Christian Church—
who teach that Yeshua the Messiah came to abolish the Torah—
will be considered "least" by Him. Not only have *too many* failed
to contemplate the meaning of the wider implications of this
word, but too many have probably also been responsible for
helping people disregard the necessity of keeping God's
commandments—in essence, obeying God. This is severely
complicated today in an American evangelical Christianity
which is being largely split over issues regarding post-
modernism and how to be relevant to our culture. With the
moral compass of the Torah largely not considered,
conservatives and those who are not-so-conservative, often do
not know what to do. It is perfectly legitimate to question
whether or not disregarding or dismissing the Torah's
instruction has truly "empowered" the Church; **because it
should be patently obvious that it has not.** When outsiders from
Judaism see this, it only keeps them away from wanting to
consider the gospel—especially if our gospel does not involve
any kind of obedience to God.[79]

Obviously, we should not be so simplistic so as to think that
the Church has never had any regard for the high standards of
the Torah. On the contrary, many holiness and piety movements
over the centuries have based their very founding on the
morality and ethics of the Torah. These people, not being Jewish,
simply did not consider ordinances such as the *moedim* or dietary
laws to apply to them.

Today's emerging Messianic community has come onto the
scene to show that there is a better way. We need not think that
belief in Yeshua the Messiah and obedience to God's
commandments are mutually exclusive. On the contrary, as
demonstrated by the life of Abraham, belief in God is to be
coupled with action reflecting the trust that we place in Him.
Likewise, if we are to truly understand the Torah obedience of
Yeshua and His Apostles, we need to be engaged with the
Apostolic Scriptures and place what they tell us into their First

---

[79] For a further and most thorough discussion of this issue, consult the
author's book *The New Testament Validates Torah.*

Century context. When we do this, we see that Yeshua and the Apostles very much lived within the normative, mainline Jewish culture of their time. This not only includes the Twelve Apostles, but also the Apostle Paul—one who is commonly misquoted and vilified as being anti-Law—when in actuality he just offered unique and innovative solutions as the gospel message expanded beyond the borders of Judea and encountered other cultures and societies.

The biggest argument that the Messianic movement can offer before Jews regarding the changing power of Yeshua—and indeed His Messiahship—is for us to live transformed lives in obedience to Him. This obedience need not be a rote observance of the commandments with little or no love, joy, peace, or even true enjoyment. This obedience needs to be a reflection of the great supernatural change that has been enacted within us because we have placed our trust in Yeshua. As Paul so astutely says, "For we are His workmanship, created in Messiah Yeshua for good works, which God prepared beforehand so that we would walk in them" (Ephesians 2:10). Our good works, just as the Lord says (Matthew 5:16), are to be seen by others **because they are a more significant testimony of what has been enacted within us** than any theological argument we can muster.

If our faith community truly has a burden for the salvation of the Jewish people, then we all need to understand that Jews have been burdened for centuries with arguments about why they should "believe in Christ." Many of these arguments have not been delivered in a spirit of reasoned and constructive dialogue. The best way to convert a Jewish person to the truth of the gospel—*and indeed convert any person*—is by living a transformed life of faith. You will be able to testify *by your actions*, that you reflect the character of Yeshua the Messiah, and that you embody the ethos of the Torah which He came to uphold. Letting your life in Messiah witness to Jewish people will help them more than handing out tracts, trying to get them engaged in some kind of "Torah discussion," or even supporting the State of Israel. **This is what the Messianic movement needs to learn how to do.** And undeniably, many Christians who see the moral decline in the Church will likewise be living this kind of life in the not-too-distant future (because this is the *same way* that they will be convinced that the Torah is important.)

What other doors has the anti-missionary influence (finally) opened?

The influence that the Jewish anti-missionaries have had in sectors of the Messianic community is very insidious. It is a move of the enemy to do nothing less than to take people away from saving faith in Yeshua the Messiah. It is a movement that has a specific agenda that we must learn to properly combat in the days ahead. But what few of us often realize, is that the anti-missionary movement *has actually performed a necessary service* for today's Messianic movement. **It is going to force us out of our theological complacency** and to join into the wider "conversation" of Biblical Studies, at least in terms of the issues that we can no longer afford to avoid or ignore.

Accepting lightweight arguments against Yeshua's Messiahship can lead a person to accepting other lightweight arguments as they relate *specifically* to the reliability of the Tanach or Old Testament itself. As a ministry, we can already document several cases where Christian individuals have: (1) entered into the Messianic movement and embraced a lifestyle of Torah observance, (2) denied the Divinity of Yeshua, **(3) denied the Messiahship of Yeshua**, and then (4) denied the existence of God Himself. Certainly, I do not want to suggest that these kinds of things do not happen in the Christian Church; they do, as there are former Christians who have denied Jesus, but perhaps in not such an interesting way. Those who deny Yeshua in the Church often go straight to atheism. Former Messianics who eventually go to atheism actually end often up as atheists because they originally sought after "Truth" with a capital T,[80] and they were led down a path straight to Hell.

Knowing that there are cases where denying Yeshua's Messiahship has later led to people denying *other things*, I would ask you to take a serious look at the following list of issues that the anti-missionary movement has opened up for us. Not unlike

---

[80] Consult the author's article "Have You Met My Friend, 'Truth'?"

discovering an Egyptian tomb in the Valley of the Kings, the tomb known as "the anti-missionary movement" is interconnected to a variety of other tombs. Ironically enough, *all* of these issues pertain directly to the reliability of the Hebrew Tanach, and are issues that the anti-missionaries themselves would certainly not be willing to discuss:

- the influence of higher criticism on Tanach/Old Testament studies
- the historicity of Israel's monarchy during the reign of King David
- the historicity of the Conquest of Canaan
- the reliability of Mosaic authorship/composition of the Pentateuch, versus the JEDP documentary hypothesis
- the historicity of the Exodus, when lack of Egyptian records for it is taken into consideration
- the historicity of the Flood, and whether it was global or regional to the Ancient Near East
- the role of Ancient Near Eastern mythology in the formation of Pentateuchal narratives
- Young Earth Creationism versus Old Earth Creationism versus Theistic Evolution
- **Theism versus Atheism**

Because of the cases of where people denying Yeshua have later denied God Himself, all issues regarding the reliability of the Bible and the events it records, the composition of His Creation and human beings, and indeed His very existence—have just been opened as a direct result of the anti-missionary movement. I would dare say that most Messianics—either laypersons *or* leaders—are really *not* ready for this. Yet, these are not new issues to consider at all, many of which are centuries-old debates. These issues present questions that anyone in theological studies has had to consider at one time or another. These are issues that can be dealt with in a reasonable manner, as the validity of Scripture can be confirmed. **They are the issues that today's Messianic movement can no longer avoid.** When considering Yeshua's Messiahship, *and the other things it is* *connected to,* are we going to do what we normally do—cover our ears and hide under our beds?

Today's Messianic movement is about four decades old, and for a forty-year old or so movement we have significant progress to make in some areas. **We do *not* need to be known as a movement that takes people away from God.** As of today, Outreach Israel Ministries and TNN Online have been part of only a handful of Messianics to address the above issues in any kind of detail, and most of the references to these issues have thus far been only in passing. These issues are *not discussed* at the vast majority of Messianic "Torah studies"—and most Messianic "Torah teachers" we have encountered do not even know about them.[81] *This is going to change in the future.* If we are truly a move that God is going to use to make a difference not only for Jewish people who need to know the Jewish Messiah, but also Christians who want to live holy lives, then we will need to be prepared to address all the issues of the times and have answers that uphold the Bible.

In a way, we can thank the anti-missionary movement for helping us to see that we have been theologically complacent. Sometimes in a true move of God, the Lord must use dramatic means to wake people out of their slumber, get them to focus on the work He has assigned, and for them to then be empowered to make a difference. Only by addressing these subjects can the Messianic movement become more theologically mature and stable. Likewise, by addressing these subjects we will be able to reach out to a world that has questions, not just about the "New Testament" and the life of Yeshua of Nazareth, but also the "Old Testament" and why they have been placed here on Earth.

The current fundamental attitude that dominates much of Messianic Biblical examination will inevitably give way to one that will actually engage and dialogue with the issues, considering and discussing their (greater) significance. Our answer for the criticisms of the History Channel or Discovery Channel will no longer be turning off or throwing away the

---

[81] Consult the author's article "Addressing the Frequently Avoided Issues Messianics Encounter in the Torah."

television, but will actually be spent considering the arguments, data, and indeed the motives of those involved. This is what we have had to do with the anti-missionary movement, *and it is only the beginning of what lies ahead.* While we have a great deal of work ahead of ourselves, we actually have a great deal of things to look forward to, because we can really be used by God to not only see people come to faith—but live lives that experience His complete *shalom*.

Once a person has denied Yeshua's Messiahship, the only other thing one can deny is the existence of God Himself. Will another installment, something like "Answering the 'Frequently Avoided Questions' About the Bible," be needed? I sincerely hope not, but the possibility remains certain. **But what is going to be necessary is for us to realize that God wants to get our attention.** When people question the Messiahship of Yeshua, doubting who He is, it signals that we need to truly realize that we are in a spiritual war for the souls of human beings. We need to be prepared for the other things that the enemy will lodge at us that will take people further and further toward eternal punishment.

About the Author

John Kimball McKee is the founder and principal writer for TNN Online, an Internet website that specializes in a wide variety of Biblical topics. He has grown up in a family that has been in constant pursuit of God's truth, and has been exposed to things of the Lord since infancy. Since 1995 he has come to the realization of the post-tribulational return of the Messiah for His own and the importance of our Hebraic Roots. He is a graduate of the University of Oklahoma (Class of 2003) with a B.A. in political science, and holds an M.A. in Biblical Studies from Asbury Theological Seminary (Class of 2009). He is a 2009 recipient of the Zondervan Biblical Languages Award for Greek. John holds memberships in the Evangelical Theological Society, the Evangelical Philosophical Society, and Christians for Biblical Equality, and is a longtime supporter of the perspectives and views of the Creationist ministry of Reasons to Believe.

John is an apologist for the Creator God and in helping people understand their faith heritage in Ancient Israel and Second Temple Judaism. Much of his ministry in the past has been campus based to the multitudes in evangelical Christianity who are associated with a wide variety of Protestant denominations and persuasions. John has introduced college students to things that are Messianic such as the original Hebrew name of our Savior, Yeshua HaMashiach (Jesus the Messiah), a name that he has known since 1983.

John's testimony before his Christian friends at college challenged much of their previous thinking about the whole of the Holy Scriptures and the need to follow the commandments of the Most High. His college peers asked him many questions: Why do you not believe in the pre-trib rapture? What do you think of the *Left Behind* books? Why do you observe the seventh-day Sabbath? Why do you eat kosher? Why do you wear a beard? Why do you celebrate the feasts of Israel? Why will you use a *tallit* and wrap *tefillin*/phylacteries during private prayer? Why do you consult original Hebrew and Greek language texts of the Bible? Why don't you come to church with us on Sunday? This led John into Messianic apologetics and the defense of our faith. John strives to be one who is committed to a life of holiness and methodical Bible study, as a person who has a testimony of being born again and who sincerely desires to obey the Lord.

As the editor of TNN Online, John's ministry has capitalized on the Internet's ability to reach people all over this planet. The Theology News Network speaks with challenging, provocative, and apologetic articles to a wide Messianic audience, and those Christians who are interested in Messianic beliefs. In the past decade (2005-2014), TNN Online has significantly emerged as a well-needed, moderate and Centrist voice, in a Messianic movement that is trying to determine its purpose, relevance, and mission to modern society—a voice which strives to sit above much of the posturing, maneuvering, and religious politics of the broad Messianic spectrum. Given his generational family background in evangelical Christian ministry, as well as in academics and the military, John carries a strong burden to assist in the development and maturation of our emerging Messianic theology and spirituality, so that we might truly know the mission of God. John has had the profound opportunity since 1997 to engage many in dialogue, so that they will consider the questions he postulates, as his only agenda is to be as Scripturally sound as possible. John believes in demonstrating a great deal of honor and respect to both his evangelical Christian, Wesleyan and Reformed heritage, as well as to the Jewish Synagogue, and together allowing the strengths and virtues of both Judaism and Christianity to be employed for the Lord's plan for the Messianic movement in the long term future.

J.K. McKee is author of numerous books, dealing with a wide range of topics that are important for today's Messianic Believers. He has also written many articles on theological issues, and is presently focusing his attention on Messianic commentaries of various books of the Bible.

J.K. McKee is the son of the late K. Kimball McKee (1951-1992) and Margaret Jeffries McKee Huey (1953-), and stepson of William Mark Huey (1951-), who married his mother in 1994, and is the executive director of Outreach Israel Ministries.

John has a very strong appreciation for those who have preceded him. His father, Kimball McKee, was a licensed lay minister in the Kentucky Conference of the United Methodist Church, and was a very strong evangelical Christian, most appreciable of the Hebraic and Jewish Roots of the faith. Among his many ministry pursuits, Kim brought the Passover *seder* to Christ United Methodist Church in Florence, KY, was a Sunday school teacher, and was extremely active in the Walk to Emmaus, leading the first men's walk in Madras, India in 1991. John is the grandson of the late William W. Jeffries (1914-1989), who served as a professor at the United States Naval Academy in Annapolis, MD from 1942-1989, notably as the museum director and founder of what is now the William W. Jeffries Memorial Archives in the Nimitz Library. John is the great-grandson of Bishop Marvin A. Franklin (1894-1972), who served as a minister and bishop of the Methodist Church, throughout his ministry serving churches in Georgia, Florida, Alabama, and Mississippi. Bishop Franklin was President of the Council of Bishops from 1959-1960. John is also the third cousin of the late Charles L. Allen (1913-2005), formerly the senior pastor of Grace Methodist Church of Atlanta, GA and First Methodist Church of Houston, TX, and author of numerous books, notably including *God's Psychiatry*. Among all of his forbearers, though, he considers his personality to be most derived from his late paternal grandfather, George Kenneth McKee (1903-1978), and his maternal grandmother, Mary Ruth Franklin Jeffries (1919-).

J.K. McKee is a native of the Northern Kentucky/Greater Cincinnati, OH area. He has also lived in Dallas, TX, Norman, OK, Kissimmee-St. Cloud, FL, and Roatán, Honduras, Central America. He presently resides in Dallas, TX, and is a member in good standing at Eitz Chaim Messianic Jewish Synagogue.

On social media, J.K. McKee can be friended on Facebook at **facebook.com/JKMMessianic**, and followed on Twitter **@JKMMessianic**.

Bibliography

Articles

Alden, Robert L. "'ādôn," in *TWOT*.

Burge, G.M. "'I am' Sayings," in *Dictionary of Jesus and the Gospels*.

Evans, C.A. "Typology," in *Dictionary of Jesus and the Gospels*.

Fuchs, E. "*sēmeron*," in *TDNT*.

Gray, J. "Molech, Moloch," in *IDB*.

Guthrie, D., and R.P. Martin. "God: God as Father (2.2)," in *Dictionary of Paul and His Letters*.

Hartley, John E. "יָשַׁע," in *TWOT*.

Hegg, Tim. (n.d.). *Psalm 22:16 — "like a lion" or "they pierced"? Torah Resource.* Retrieved 07 October, 2007, from <http://www.torahresource.com>.

_____. (2006). *In the Name of the Father and the Son and the Holy Spirit: Matt 28:19 – A Later Addition to Matthew's Gospel? Torah Resource.* Retrieved 14 October, 2011, from <http://www.torahresource.com>.

Hurtado, L.W. "Lord," in *Dictionary of Paul and His Letters*.

Kaiser, Walter C. "עָבַד," in *TWOT*.

Kleinknecht, H. "*theíotēs*," in *TDNT*.

Marshall, I.H. "Son of Man," in *Dictionary of Jesus and the Gospels*.

Meyer, M.W. "Master," in *ISBE*.

Millam, John. (n.d.). *The Genesis Genealogies. Reasons to Believe.* Retrieved 14 October, 2007, from <http://www.reasons.org>.

Rengstorf, K.H. "*despótēs*," in *TDNT*.

Revell, E.J. "Masoretic Text," in *ABD*.

Stauffer, E. "*heís*," in *TDNT*.

Witherington III, B. "Lord," in *Dictionary of Jesus and the Gospels*.

Wolf, Herbert, "אחד," in *TWOT*.

Stauffer, E. "*theótēs*," in *TDNT*.

"Virgin Birth of Christ," in *Baker Encyclopedia of Christian Apologetics*.

Yamauchi, Edwin. "חָוָה," in *TWOT*.

Bible Versions and Study Bibles

Abegg, Jr., Martin, Peter Flint, and Eugene Ulrich, trans. *The Dead Sea Scrolls Bible* (New York: HarperCollins, 1999).

American Standard Version (New York: Thomas Nelson & Sons, 1901).

Barker, Kenneth L., ed., et. al. *NIV Study Bible* (Grand Rapids: Zondervan, 2002).

Berlin, Adele, and Marc Zvi Brettler, eds. *The Jewish Study Bible* (Oxford: Oxford University Press, 2004).

Bratcher, Robert G., ed. *Good News Bible: The Bible in Today's English Version* (New York: American Bible Society, 1976).

Esposito, Paul W. *The Apostles' Bible, An English Septuagint Version* (http://www.apostlesbible.com/).

Garrett, Duane A., ed., et. al. *NIV Archaeological Study Bible* (Grand Rapids: Zondervan, 2005).

Green, Jay P., trans. *The Interlinear Bible* (Lafayette, IN: Sovereign Grace Publishers, 1986).

Green, Joel B., ed. *The Wesley Study Bible* (Nashville: Abingdon, 2009).

God's Game Plan: The Athlete's Bible 2007, HCSB (Nashville: Serendipity House Publishers, 2007).

Harrelson, Walter J., ed., et. al. *New Interpreter's Study Bible*, NRSV (Nashville: Abingdon, 2003).

Harris, W. Hall, ed. *The Holy Bible: The Net Bible*, New English Translation (Dallas: Biblical Studies Press, 2001).

Holman Christian Standard Bible (Nashville: Broadman & Holman, 2004).

Holy Bible, King James Version (edited 1789).

Holy Bible, New International Version (Grand Rapids: Zondervan, 1978).

LaHaye, Tim, ed. *Tim LaHaye Prophecy Study Bible*, KJV (Chattanooga: AMG Publishers, 2000).

Lattimore, Richmond, trans. *The New Testament* (New York: North Point Press, 1996).

May, Herbert G., and Bruce M. Metzger, eds. *The New Oxford Annotated Bible With the Apocrypha*, RSV (New York: Oxford University Press, 1977).

Meeks, Wayne A., ed., et. al. *The HarperCollins Study Bible*, NRSV (New York: HarperCollins, 1993).

Newman, Barclay M., ed. *Holy Bible: Contemporary English Version* (New York: American Bible Society, 1995).

New American Standard Bible (La Habra, CA: Foundation Press Publications, 1971).

New American Standard, Updated Edition (Anaheim, CA: Foundation Publications, 1995).

New English Bible (Oxford and Cambridge: Oxford and Cambridge University Presses, 1970).

New King James Version (Nashville: Thomas Nelson, 1982).

New Revised Standard Version (National Council of Churches of Christ, 1989).

Packer, J.I., ed. *The Holy Bible, English Standard Version* (Wheaton, IL: Crossway Bibles, 2001).

Peterson, Eugene H. *The Message: The Bible in Contemporary Language* (Colorado Springs: NavPress, 2002).

Phillips, J.B., trans. *The New Testament in Modern English* (New York: Touchstone, 1972).

Pietersma, Albert, and Benjamin G. Wright, eds. *A New English Translation of the Septuagint* (Oxford and New York: Oxford University Press, 2007).

Ryrie, Charles C., ed. *The Ryrie Study Bible*, NASB (Chicago: Moody Press, 1978).

Scherman, Nosson, and Meir Zlotowitz, eds. *ArtScroll Tanach* (Brooklyn: Mesorah Publications, 1996).

Siewert, Frances E., ed. *The Amplified Bible* (Grand Rapids: Zondervan, 1965).

Suggs, M. Jack, and Katharine Doob Sakenfeld, and James R. Mueller, et. al. *The Oxford Study Bible*, REB (New York: Oxford University Press, 1992).

Stern, David H., trans. *Jewish New Testament* (Clarksville, MD: Jewish New Testament Publications, 1995).

_____, trans. *Complete Jewish Bible* (Clarksville, MD: Jewish New Testament Publications, 1998).

Tanakh: The Holy Scriptures (Philadelphia: Jewish Publication Society, 1999).

The Holy Bible, Revised Standard Version (Nashville: Cokesbury, 1952).

The Jerusalem Bible (Jerusalem: Koren Publishers, 2000).

Today's New International Version (Grand Rapids: Zondervan, 2005).

Tree of Life Messianic Family Bible—New Covenant (Shippensburg, PA: Destiny Image, 2011).

Williams, Charles B., trans. *The New Testament: A Private Translation in the Language of the People* (Chicago: Moody Publishers, 1937).

Wright, N.T. *The Kingdom New Testament: A Contemporary Translation* (New York: HarperCollins, 2011).

Young, Robert, trans. *Young's Literal Translation.*

Zodhiates, Spiros, ed. *Hebrew-Greek Key Study Bible*, NASB (Chattanooga: AMG Publishers, 1994).

Books

Bauckham, Richard. *Jesus and the God of Israel* (Grand Rapids: Eerdmans, 2008).

Berkowitz, Ariel and D'vorah. *Torah Rediscovered* (Lakewood, CO: First Fruits of Zion, 1996).

_____. *Take Hold* (Littleton, CO: First Fruits of Zion, 1999).

Bowman, Robert M., Jr., and J. Ed Komoszewski. *Putting Jesus in His Place: The Case for the Deity of Christ* (Grand Rapids: Kregel, 2007).

Brown, Michael L. *Answering Jewish Objections to Jesus, Volume 1: General and Historical Objections* (Grand Rapids: Baker Books, 2000).

_____. *Answering Jewish Objections to Jesus, Volume 2: Theological Objections* (Grand Rapids: Baker Books, 2000).

_____. *Answering Jewish Objections to Jesus, Volume 3: Messianic Prophecy Objections* (Grand Rapids: Baker Books, 2003).

Bruce, F.F. *New Testament History* (New York: Doubleday, 1969).

Carson, D.A., and Douglas J. Moo. *An Introduction to the New Testament,* second edition (Grand Rapids: Zondervan, 2005).

Cohn-Sherbok, Dan, ed. *Voices of Messianic Judaism* (Baltimore: Lederer Books, 2001).

Dillard, Raymond B., and Tremper Longman III. *An Introduction to the Old Testament* (Grand Rapids: Zondervan, 1994).

Erickson, Millard J. *Making Sense of the Trinity: Three Crucial Questions* (Grand Rapids: Baker Books, 2000).

Fee, Gordon D., and Douglas Stuart. *How to Read the Bible for All Its Worth* (Grand Rapids: Zondervan, 2003).

Fischer, John, ed. *The Enduring Paradox: Exploratory Essays in Messianic Judaism* (Baltimore: Lederer, 2000).

Friedman, David. *They Loved the Torah* (Baltimore: Lederer Books, 2001).

Gundry, Robert H. *A Survey of the New Testament,* third edition (Grand Rapids: Zondervan, 1994).

Guthrie, Donald. *New Testament Introduction* (Downers Grove, IL: InterVarsity, 1990).

Harrison, R.K. *Introduction to the Old Testament* (Grand Rapids: Eerdmans, 1969).

Hegg, Tim. *The Letter Writer: Paul's Background and Torah Perspective* (Littleton, CO: First Fruits of Zion, 2002).

_____. *Messiah in the Tanach* (Tacoma, WA: TorahResource, 2003).

_____. *The Messiah: Introduction to Christology* (Tacoma, WA: TorahResource, 2006).

Hurtado, Larry W. *Lord Jesus Christ: Devotion to Jesus in Earliest Christianity* (Grand Rapids: Eerdmans, 2003).

Juster, Daniel C. *Jewish Roots* (Shippensburg, PA: Destiny Image, 1995).

Kaiser, Walter C. *Toward Old Testament Ethics* (Grand Rapids: Zondervan, 1983).

_____. *The Messiah in the Old Testament* (Grand Rapids: Zondervan, 1995).

_____. *The Promise-Plan of God: A Biblical Theology of the Old and New Testaments* (Grand Rapids: Zondervan, 2008).

Kaiser, Walter C., and Moisés Silva. *An Introduction to Biblical Hermeneutics* (Grand Rapids: Zondervan, 1994).

Kitchen, K.A. *Ancient Orient and Old Testament* (Madison, WI: InterVarsity, 1966).

McGrath, Alister E. *Christian Theology: An Introduction* (Oxford: Blackwell Publishing, 2001).

McKee, J.K. *Torah In the Balance, Volume I* (Kissimmee, FL: TNN Press, 2003).

_____. *The New Testament Validates Torah* (Kissimmee, FL: TNN Press, 2004).

_____. *James for the Practical Messianic* (Kissimmee, FL: TNN Press, 2005).

_____. *Hebrews for the Practical Messianic* (Kissimmee, FL: TNN Press, 2006).

_____. *A Survey of the Apostolic Scriptures for the Practical Messianic* (Kissimmee, FL: TNN Press, 2006).

_____. *Philippians for the Practical Messianic* (Kissimmee, FL: TNN Press, 2007).

_____. *Galatians for the Practical Messianic*, second edition (Kissimmee, FL: TNN Press, 2007).

_____. *Ephesians for the Practical Messianic* (Kissimmee, FL: TNN Press, 2008).

_____. *A Survey of the Tanach for the Practical Messianic* (Kissimmee, FL: TNN Press, 2008).

_____. *Colossians and Philemon for the Practical Messianic* (Kissimmee, FL: TNN Press, 2010).

_____. *Acts 15 for the Practical Messianic* (Kissimmee, FL: TNN Press, 2010).

_____. *The Pastoral Epistles for the Practical Messianic* (Kissimmee, FL: TNN Press, 2012).

Moseley, Ron. *Yeshua: A Guide to the Real Jesus and the Original Church* (Baltimore: Lederer Books, 1996).

Patzia, Arthur G. *The Making of the New Testament: Origin, Collection, Text & Canon* (Downers Grove, IL: InterVarsity, 1995).

Rydelnik, Michael. *The Messianic Hope: Is the Hebrew Bible Messianic?* (Nashville: B&H Publishing Group, 2010).

Strickland, Wayne G., ed. *Five Views on Law and Gospel* (Grand Rapids: Zondervan, 1996).

Thompson, David L. *Bible Study That Works* (Nappanee, IN: Evangel Publishing House, 1994).

Tidball, Derek. *The Message of the Cross* (Downers Grove, IL: InterVarsity, 2001).

Unger, Merrill F. *Unger's Bible Handbook* (Chicago: Moody Press, 1967).

Wilson, Marvin R. *Our Father Abraham* (Grand Rapids: Eerdmans, 1989).

Wright, N.T. *Paul in Fresh Perspective* (Minneapolis: Fortress Press, 2005).

Christian Reference Sources and Cited Commentaries

Alexander, T. Desmond, and David W. Baker, eds. *Dictionary of the Old Testament Pentateuch* (Downers Grove, IL: InterVarsity, 2003).

Arnold, Bill T., and H.G.M. Williamson, eds. *Dictionary of the Old Testament Historical Books* (Downers Grove, IL: InterVarsity, 2005).

Bercot, David W., ed. *A Dictionary of Early Christian Beliefs* (Peabody, MA: Hendrickson, 1998).

Bromiley, Geoffrey, ed. *International Standard Bible Encyclopedia*, 4 vols. (Grand Rapids: Eerdmans, 1988).

Bruce, F.F. *The Gospel of John* (Grand Rapids: Eerdmans, 1983).

Buttrick, George, ed. et. al. *The Interpreter's Dictionary of the Bible*, 4 vols. (Nashville: Abingdon, 1962).

Cairns, Alan. *Dictionary of Theological Terms* (Greenville, SC: Ambassador Emerald International, 2002).

Carson, D.A. "Matthew," in Frank E. Gaebelein, ed. et. al. *Expositor's Bible Commentary* (Grand Rapids: Zondervan, 1984), 8:3-599.

_____. *Pillar New Testament Commentary: The Gospel According to John* (Grand Rapids: Eerdmans, 1991).

Craigie, Peter C. *New International Commentary on the Old Testament: The Book of Deuteronomy* (Grand Rapids: Eerdmans, 1976).

Cranfield, C.E.B. *International Critical Commentary: Romans 9-16* (London: T&T Clark, 1979).

Crim, Keith, ed. *Interpreter's Dictionary of the Bible: Supplementary Volume* (Nashville: Abingdon, 1976).

Edwards, James R. *Pillar New Testament Commentary: The Gospel According to Mark* (Grand Rapids: Eerdmans, 2002).

Evans, Craig A., and Stanley E. Porter, eds. *Dictionary of New Testament Background* (Downers Grove, IL: InterVarsity, 2000).

Fee, Gordon D. *New International Commentary on the New Testament: The First Epistle to the Corinthians* (Grand Rapids: Eerdmans, 1987).

France, R.T. *New International Commentary on the New Testament: The Gospel of Matthew* (Grand Rapids: Eerdmans, 2007).

Freedman, David Noel, ed. *Anchor Bible Dictionary*, 6 vols. (New York: Doubleday, 1992).

_____, ed. *Eerdmans Dictionary of the Bible* (Grand Rapids: Eerdmans, 2000).

Geisler, Norman L., ed. *Baker Encyclopedia of Christian Apologetics* (Grand Rapids: Baker, 1999).

Green, Joel B., Scot McKnight, and I. Howard Marshall, eds. *Dictionary of Jesus and the Gospels* (Downers Grove, IL: InterVarsity, 1992).

Grenz, Stanley J., David Guretzki, and Cherith Fee Nordling. *Pocket Dictionary of Theological Terms* (Downers Grove, IL: InterVarsity, 1999).

Harrison, Everett F., ed. *Baker's Dictionary of Theology* (Grand Rapids: Baker Book House, 1960).

Hawthorne, Gerald F., Ralph P. Martin, and Daniel G. Reid, eds. *Dictionary of Paul and His Letters* (Downers Grove, IL: InterVarsity, 1993).

Kalland, Earl. S. "Deuteronomy," in Frank E. Gaebelein, ed. et. al. *Expositor's Bible Commentary* (Grand Rapids: Zondervan, 1992), 3:3-235.

Kruse, Colin G. *Tyndale New Testament Commentaries: John* (Grand Rapids: Eerdmans, 2003).

Lane, William L. *New International Commentary on the New Testament: The Gospel According to Mark* (Grand Rapids: Eerdmans, 1974).

Liefield, Walter L. "Luke," in *EXP*, 8:797-1059.

Longman III, Tremper, and Peter Enns, eds. *Dictionary of the Old Testament Wisdom, Poetry & Writings* (Downers Grove, IL: InterVarsity, 2008).

Martin, Ralph P., and Peter H. Davids, eds. *Dictionary of the Later New Testament & its Developments* (Downers Grove, IL: InterVarsity, 1997).

McLay, R. Timothy. *The Use of the Septuagint in New Testament Research* (Grand Rapids: Eerdmans, 2003).

Milne, Bruce. *The Message of John* (Downers Grove, IL: InterVarsity, 1993).

Moo, Douglas J. *Pillar New Testament Commentary: The Letters to the Colossians and to Philemon* (Grand Rapids: Eerdmans, 2008).

Morris, Leon. *New International Commentary on the New Testament: The Gospel According to John* (Grand Rapids: Eerdmans, 1971).

Motyer, J.A. *The Message of James* (Downers Grove, IL: InterVarsity, 1985).

Nolland, John. *New International Greek Testament Commentary: The Gospel of Matthew* (Grand Rapids: Eerdmans, 2005),

Patzia, Arthur G., and Anthony J. Petrotta. *Pocket Dictionary of Biblical Studies* (Downers Grove, IL: InterVarsity, 2002).

Roberts, Alexander, and James Donaldson, eds. *The Apostolic Fathers,* American Edition.

Schaff, Philip. *History of the Christian Church,* 8 vols. (Grand Rapids: Eerdmans, 1995).

Tenney, Merrill C., ed. *The New International Dictionary of the Bible* (Grand Rapids: Zondervan, 1987).

Thompson, J.A. *Tyndale Old Testament Commentaries: Deuteronomy* (Downers Grove, IL: InterVarsity, 1974).

The Book of Common Prayer (New York: Oxford University Press, 1990).

Von Rad, Gerhard. *Deuteronomy: A Commentary* (Philadelphia: Westminster Press, 1966).

Greek Language Resources

Aland, Kurt, et. al. *The Greek New Testament, Fourth Revised Edition* (Stuttgart: Deutche Bibelgesellschaft/United Bible Societies, 1998).

Brenton, Sir Lancelot C. L., ed & trans. *The Septuagint With Apocrypha* (Peabody, MA: Hendrickson, 1999).

Bromiley, Geoffrey W., ed. *Theological Dictionary of the New Testament,* abridged (Grand Rapids: Eerdmans, 1985).

Brown, Robert K., and Philip W. Comfort, trans. *The New Greek-English Interlinear New Testament* (Carol Stream, IL: Tyndale House, 1990).

Danker, Frederick William, ed., et. al. *A Greek-English Lexicon of the New Testament and Other Early Christian Literature,* third edition (Chicago: University of Chicago Press, 2000).

Liddell, H.G., and R. Scott. *An Intermediate Greek-English Lexicon* (Oxford: Clarendon Press, 1994).

Metzger, Bruce M. *A Textual Commentary on the Greek New Testament* (London and New York: United Bible Societies, 1975).

Nestle, Erwin, and Kurt Aland, eds. *Novum Testamentum Graece, Nestle-Aland 27th Edition* (New York: American Bible Society, 1993).

Nestle-Aland Greek-English New Testament, NE27-RSV (Stuttgart: United Bible Societies/Deutche Bibelgesellschaft, 2001).

Newman, Jr., Barclay M. *A Concise Greek-English Dictionary of the New Testament* (Stuttgart: United Bible Societies/Deutche Bibelgesellschaft, 1971).

Rahlfs, Alfred, ed. *Septuaginta* (Stuttgart: Deutsche Bibelgesellschaft, 1979).

Rogers, Cleon L., Jr., and Cleon L. Rogers III. *The New Linguistic and Exegetical Key to the Greek New Testament* (Grand Rapids: Zondervan, 1998).

Thayer, Joseph H. *Thayer's Greek-English Lexicon of the New Testament* (Peabody, MA: Hendrickson, 2003).

Vine, W.E. *Vine's Expository Dictionary of New Testament Words* (Nashville: Thomas Nelson, 1968).

Wallace, Daniel B. *Greek Grammar Beyond the Basics* (Grand Rapids: Zondervan, 1996).

Zodhiates, Spiros, ed. *Complete Word Study Dictionary: New Testament* (Chattanooga: AMG Publishers, 1993).

Hebrew Language Resources

Arnold, Bill T., and John H. Choi. *A Guide to Biblical Hebrew Syntax* (New York: Cambridge University Press, 2003).

Baker, Warren, and Eugene Carpenter, eds. *Complete Word Study Dictionary: Old Testament* (Chattanooga: AMG Publishers, 2003).

Brown, Francis, S.R. Driver, and Charles A. Briggs. *Hebrew and English Lexicon of the Old Testament* (Oxford: Clarendon Press, 1979).

Davidson, Benjamin. *The Analytical Hebrew and Chaldee Lexicon* (Grand Rapids: Zondervan, 1970).

Dotan, Aron, ed. *Biblia Hebraica Leningradensia* (Peabody, MA: Hendrickson, 2001).

Elliger, Karl, and Wilhelm Rudolph, et. al., eds. *Biblica Hebraica Stuttgartensia* (Stuttgart: Deutche Bibelgesellschaft, 1977).

Gabe, Eric S., ed. *New Testament in Hebrew and English* (Hitchin, UK: Society for Distributing the Hebrew Scriptures, 2000).

Harris, R. Laird, Gleason L. Archer, Jr., and Bruce K. Waltke, eds. *Theological Wordbook of the Old Testament* (Chicago: Moody Press, 1980).

Holladay, William L., ed. *A Concise Hebrew and Aramaic Lexicon of the Old Testament* (Leiden, the Netherlands: E.J. Brill, 1988).

Jastrow, Marcus. *Dictionary of the Targumim, Talmud Bavli, Talmud Yerushalmi, and Midrashic Literature* (New York: Judaica Treasury, 2004).

Kelley, Page H., Daniel S. Mynatt, and Timothy G. Crawford, eds. *The Masorah of Biblia Hebraica Stuttgartensia* (Grand Rapids: Eerdmans, 1998).

Koehler, Ludwig, and Walter Baumgartner, eds. *The Hebrew & Aramaic Lexicon of the Old Testament*, 2 vols. (Leiden, the Netherlands: Brill, 2001).

Seow, C.L. *A Grammar for Biblical Hebrew*, revised edition (Nashville: Abingdon, 1995).

Tov, Emanuel. *Textual Criticism of the Hebrew Bible* (Minneapolis: Fortress Press, 1992).

תורה נביאים כתובים והברית החדשה (Jerusalem: Bible Society in Israel, 1991).

Unger, Merrill F., and William White. *Nelson's Expository Dictionary of the Old Testament* (Nashville: Thomas Nelson, 1980).

Historical Sources and Ancient Literature

Bettenson, Henry, and Chris Maunder, eds. *Documents of the Christian Church* (Oxford: Oxford University Press, 1999).

Eusebius of Caesarea: *Ecclesiastical History*, trans. C.F. Cruse (Peabody, MA: Hendrickson, 1998).

González, Justo L. *The Story of Christianity*, Vol. 1 (San Francisco: Harper Collins, 1984).

_____. *The Story of Christianity*, Vol. 2 (San Francisco: HarperCollins, 1985).

Irvin, Dale T., and Scott W. Sunquist. *History of the World Christian Movement*, Vol. 1 (Maryknoll, NY: Orbis Books, 2001).

Josephus, Flavius: *The Works of Josephus: Complete and Unabridged*, trans. William Whiston (Peabody, MA: Hendrickson, 1987).

Judaeus, Philo: *The Works of Philo: Complete and Unabridged*, trans. C.D. Yonge (Peabody, MA: Hendrickson, 1993).

Shanks, Hershel, ed. *Ancient Israel: From Abraham to the Roman Destruction of the Temple* (Washington, D.C.: Biblical Archaeology Society, 1999).

Staniforth, Maxwell, trans. *Early Christian Writings: The Apostolic Fathers* (Harmondsworth, UK: Penguin Books, 1980).

Jewish Reference Sources and Cited Commentaries

Cohen, Abraham. *Everyman's Talmud: The Major Teachings of the Rabbinic Sages* (New York: Schoken, 1995).

Eisenberg, Ronald L. *The JPS Guide to Jewish Traditions* (Philadelphia: Jewish Publication Society, 2004).

Encyclopaedia Judaica. MS Windows 9x. Brooklyn: Judaica Multimedia (Israel) Ltd, 1997.

Frank, Daniel H., Oliver Leaman, and Charles H. Manekin, eds. *The Jewish Philosophy Reader* (London and New York: Routledge, 2000).

Friedman, Richard Elliot. *Commentary on the Torah* (New York: HarperCollins, 2001).

Harlow, Jules, ed. *Siddur Sim Shalom for Shabbat and Festivals* (New York: Rabbinical Assembly, 2007).

Hertz, J.H., ed. *Pentateuch & Haftorahs* (London: Soncino, 1960).

_____, ed. *The Authorised Daily Prayer Book*, revised (New York: Bloch Publishing Company, 1960).

Kolatch, Alfred J. *The Jewish Book of Why* (Middle Village, NY: Jonathan David Publishers, 1981).

_____. *The Second Jewish Book of Why* (Middle Village, NY: Jonathan David Publishers, 1985).

Levine, Amy-Jill, and Marc Zvi Brettler, eds. *The Jewish Annotated New Testament*, NRSV (Oxford: Oxford University Press, 2011).

Lieber, David L. *Etz Hayim: Torah and Commentary* (New York: Rabbinical Assembly, 2001).

Neusner, Jacob, trans. *The Mishnah: A New Translation* (New Haven and London: Yale University Press, 1988).

_____, ed. *The Tosefta: Translated from the Hebrew With a New Introduction*, 2 vols. (Peabody, MA: Hendrickson, 2002).

_____, and William Scott Green, eds. *Dictionary of Judaism in the Biblical Period* (Peabody, MA: Hendrickson, 2002).

Sarna, Nahum M. *JPS Torah Commentary: Genesis* (Philadelphia: Jewish Publication Society, 1989).

_____. *JPS Torah Commentary: Exodus* (Philadelphia: Jewish Publication Society, 1991).

Scherman, Nosson, ed., et. al. *The ArtScroll Chumash, Stone Edition*, 5th ed. (Brooklyn: Mesorah Publications, 2000).

Tigay, Jeffrey H. *JPS Torah Commentary: Deuteronomy* (Philadelphia: Jewish Publication Society, 1996).

Messianic Reference Sources

Hegg, Tim. *Commentary on the Gospel of Matthew: Chapters 1-7* (Tacoma, WA: TorahResource, 2007).

Kasdan, Barney. *Matthew Presents Yeshua, King Messiah: A Messianic Commentary* (Clarksville, MD: Lederer Books, 2011).

Stern, David H. *Jewish New Testament Commentary* (Clarksville, MD: Jewish New Testament Publications, 1992).

Miscellaneous Texts and Lexicons

Eby, Aaron, and Robert Morris, trans., et. al. *The Delitzsch Hebrew Gospels: A Hebrew/English Translation* (Marshfield, MO: Vine of David, 2011).

Gruber, Daniel, trans. *The Messianic Writings* (Hanover, NH: Elijah Publishing, 2011).

The Scriptures, third edition (Northriding, South Africa: Institute for Scripture Research, 2009).

Wise, Michael, Martin Abegg, Jr., and Edward Cook, trans. *The Dead Sea Scrolls: A New Translation* (San Francisco: HarperCollins, 1996).

Young, Robert. *Young's Analytical Concordance to the Bible* (Grand Rapids: Eerdmans, 1977).

Software Programs

BibleWorks 7.0. MS Windows XP. Norfolk: BibleWorks, LLC, 2006. CD-ROM.

BibleWorks 8.0. MS Windows Vista/7 Release. Norfolk: BibleWorks, LLC, 2009-2010. DVD-ROM.

E-Sword 9.9.1. MS Windows Vista/7. Franklin, TN: Equipping Ministries Foundation, 2011.

The Babylonian Talmud: A Translation and Commentary. MS Windows XP. Peabody, MA: Hendrickson, 2005. CD-ROM.

confronting issues

TNN Press is the official publishing arm of TNN Online, and its parent organization, Outreach Israel Ministries. TNN Press is dedicated to producing high quality, doctrinally sound, challenging, and fair-minded Messianic materials and resources for the Twenty-First Century. TNN Press offers a wide array of new and exciting books and resources for the truth seeker.

TNN Press titles are available for purchase at

www.outreachisrael.net or at

amazon.com

Hebraic Roots: An Introductory Study
is TNN Press' main, best-selling publication, that offers a good overview of the Messianic movement and Messianic lifestyle that can be used for individual or group study in twelve easy lessons

Introduction to Things Messianic
is an excellent companion to *Hebraic Roots*, which goes into substantially more detail into the emerging theology of the Messianic movement, specific areas of Torah observance, and aspects of faith such as salvation and eschatology

The Messianic Helper series, edited by Margaret McKee Huey, includes a series of books with instructional information on how to have a Messianic home, including holiday celebration guides. After reading both *Hebraic Roots* and *Introduction to Things Messianic,* these are the publications you need to read!

Messianic Spring Holiday Helper
is a guide to assist you during the Spring holiday season, analyzing the importance of *Purim*, Passover and Unleavened Bread, *Shavuot*, and the non-Biblical holiday of Easter

Messianic Fall Holiday Helper
is a guide for the Fall holiday season of *Yom Teruah/Rosh HaShanah*, *Yom Kippur*, and *Sukkot*, along with reflective teachings and exhortations

Messianic Winter Holiday Helper
is a guide to help you during the Winter holiday season, addressing the significance of *Chanukah*, the period of the Maccabees, and the non-Biblical holiday of Christmas

Messianic Sabbath Helper
will be a guide that will help you make the seventh-day Sabbath a delight, discussing how to keep *Shabbat*, common Jewish traditions associated with *Shabbat*, the history of the transition to Sunday that occurred in early Christianity
> already available is the five-chapter mini-book excerpt **Shabbat: Sabbath for Messianic Believers**, intended as a congregational handout

Messianic Kosher Helper
will be a guide discussing various aspects of the kosher dietary laws, clean and unclean meats, common Jewish traditions associated with kashrut, and common claims made that these are no longer important for Believers
> also available is the five-chapter mini-book excerpt **Kashrut: Kosher for Messianic Believers**, intended as a congregational handout

Messianic Torah Helper
is a guide that weighs the different perspectives of the Pentateuch present in Jewish and Christian theology, considers the role of the Law for God's people, and how today's Messianics can fairly approach issues of *halachah* and tradition in their Torah observance

Outreach Israel Ministries director **Mark Huey** has written Torah commentaries and reflections that are thought provoking and very enlightening for Messianic Believers today.

TorahScope Volume I
is a compilation workbook of insightful commentaries on the weekly Torah and Haftarah portions

TorahScope Volume II
is a second compilation workbook of expanded commentaries on the weekly Torah and Haftarah portions

TorahScope Volume III
is a third compilation workbook of expanded commentaries on the weekly Torah and Haftarah portions, specifically concentrating on the theme of faith

TorahScope Haftarah Exhortations
is a compilation workbook of insightful commentaries on the specific, weekly Haftarah portions, designed to be used to compliment the weekly Torah reading

TorahScope Apostolic Scripture Reflections
is a compilation workbook of insightful reflections on suggested readings from the Apostolic Scriptures or New Testament, designed to be used to compliment the weekly Torah and Haftarah readings

Counting the Omer: A Daily Devotional Toward Shavuot
is a daily devotional with fifty succinct reflections from Psalms, guiding you during the season between the festivals of Passover and Pentecost

Sayings of the Fathers: A Messianic Perspective on Pirkei Avot
is a daily devotional for two years of reflection on the Mishnah tractate *Pirkei Avot*, introducing you to some of the key views present in the Apostolic period as witnessed by the Jewish Sages (intended to be read during the counting of the *omer*)

TNN Online editor and Messianic apologist **J.K. McKee** has written on Messianic theology and practice, including studies on Torah observance, the end-times, and commentaries that are helpful to those who have difficult questions to answer.

The New Testament Validates Torah
Does the New Testament Really Do Away With the Law?
is a resource examining a wide variety of Biblical passages, discussing whether or not the Torah of Moses is really abolished in the New Testament

Torah In the Balance, Volume I
The Validity of the Torah and Its Practical Life Applications
examines the principal areas of a Torah observant walk of faith for the newcomer, including one's spiritual motives

Torah In the Balance, Volume II
The Set-Apart Life in Action—The Outward Expressions of Faith
will examine many of the finer areas of Torah observance, which has a diversity of interpretations and applications as witnessed in both mainstream Judaism and the wide Messianic community

Confronting Critical Issues
An Analysis of Subjects that Affects the Growth and Stability of the Emerging Messianic Movement
compiles a variety of articles and analyses that directly confront negative teachings and trends that have been witnessed in the broad Messianic community in the past decade

TNN Press has produced a variety of **Messianic commentaries** on various books of the Bible under the "for the Practical Messianic" byline. These can be used in an individual, small group, or congregational study.

general commentaries:
A Survey of the Tanach for the Practical Messianic
A Survey of the Apostolic Scriptures for the Practical Messianic

specific book commentaries:
Acts 15 for the Practical Messianic
Romans for the Practical Messianic
1 Corinthians for the Practical Messianic (coming 2015)
Galatians for the Practical Messianic
Ephesians for the Practical Messianic
Philippians for the Practical Messianic
Colossians and Philemon for the Practical Messianic
The Pastoral Epistles for the Practical Messianic
1&2 Thessalonians for the Practical Messianic
James for the Practical Messianic
Hebrews for the Practical Messianic

10926053R10100

Printed in Great Britain
by Amazon.co.uk, Ltd.,
Marston Gate.